THE BRIDE AND THE BACHELOR

by Ronald Millar

Copyright © 1958 by Ronald Millar
All Rights Reserved

THE BRIDE AND THE BACHELOR is fully protected under the copyright laws of the British Commonwealth, including Canada, the United States of America, and all other countries of the Copyright Union. All rights, including professional and amateur stage productions, recitation, lecturing, public reading, motion picture, radio broadcasting, television, online/digital production, and the rights of translation into foreign languages are strictly reserved.

ISBN 978-0-573-01054-5

concordtheatricals.co.uk
concordtheatricals.com

FOR AMATEUR PRODUCTION ENQUIRIES

UNITED KINGDOM AND WORLD
EXCLUDING NORTH AMERICA
licensing@concordtheatricals.co.uk
020-7054-7298

Each title is subject to availability from Concord Theatricals,
depending upon country of performance.

CAUTION: Professional and amateur producers are hereby warned that *THE BRIDE AND THE BACHELOR* is subject to a licensing fee. The purchase, renting, lending or use of this book does not constitute a licence to perform this title(s), which licence must be obtained from the appropriate agent prior to any performance. Performance of this title(s) without a licence is a violation of copyright law and may subject the producer and/or presenter of such performances to penalties. Both amateurs and professionals considering a production are strongly advised to apply to the appropriate agent before starting rehearsals, advertising, or booking a theatre. A licensing fee must be paid whether the title is presented for charity or gain and whether or not admission is charged.

This work is published by Samuel French, an imprint of Concord Theatricals Ltd.

The Professional Rights in this play are controlled by Eric Glass Ltd, 3rd Floor, 86-90 Paul Street, London EC2A 4NE.

No one shall make any changes in this title for the purpose of production. No part of this book may be reproduced, stored in a retrieval system, scanned, uploaded, or transmitted in any form, by any means, now known or yet to be invented, including mechanical, electronic, digital, photocopying, recording, videotaping, or otherwise, without the prior written permission of the publisher. No one shall share this title, or part of this title, to any social media or file hosting websites.

The moral right of Ronald Millar to be identified as author of this work has been asserted in accordance with Section 77 of the Copyright, Designs and Patents Act 1988.

USE OF COPYRIGHTED MUSIC

A licence issued by Concord Theatricals to perform this play does not include permission to use the incidental music specified in this publication. In the United Kingdom: Where the place of performance is already licensed by the PERFORMING RIGHT SOCIETY (PRS) a return of the music used must be made to them. If the place of performance is not so licensed then application should be made to PRS for Music (www.prsformusic.com). A separate and additional licence from PHONOGRAPHIC PERFORMANCE LTD (www.ppluk.com) may be needed whenever commercial recordings are used. Outside the United Kingdom: Please contact the appropriate music licensing authority in your territory for the rights to any incidental music.

USE OF COPYRIGHTED THIRD-PARTY MATERIALS

Licensees are solely responsible for obtaining formal written permission from copyright owners to use copyrighted third-party materials (e.g., artworks, logos) in the performance of this play and are strongly cautioned to do so. If no such permission is obtained by the licensee, then the licensee must use only original materials that the licensee owns and controls. Licensees are solely responsible and liable for clearances of all third-party copyrighted materials, and shall indemnify the copyright owners of the play(s) and their licensing agent, Concord Theatricals Ltd., against any costs, expenses, losses and liabilities arising from the use of such copyrighted third-party materials by licensees.

IMPORTANT BILLING AND CREDIT REQUIREMENTS

If you have obtained performance rights to this title, please refer to your licensing agreement for important billing and credit requirements.

THE BRIDE AND THE BACHELOR

Presented by Peter Saunders at the Duchess Theatre, London, on the 19th December 1956, with the following cast of characters—

(in the order of their appearance)

BARBARA KILPATRICK	*Margaret McCourt*
MISS BOWDEN	*Anna Turner*
ISABEL KILPATRICK	*Cicely Courtneidge*
SERENA KILPATRICK	*Jill Raymond*
BLODWEN MORGAN-JONES	*Viola Lyel*
JASON KILPATRICK	*Robertson Hare*
SIR WILLIAM BENEDICK-BARLOW	*Naunton Wayne*
JOE TILNEY	*Warren Stanhope*

Directed by CHARLES HICKMAN
Décor by MICHAEL WEIGHT

SYNOPSIS OF SCENES

The action of the play passes in the lounge hall of the Kilpatricks' house in St. John's Wood, London

ACT I

SCENE 1 About 8 p.m. on an October evening
SCENE 2 Three hours later

ACT II

A few minutes later

ACT III

About 9.45 a.m. the next morning

Time—the present

The excerpt quoted on pages 1, 2 and 3 from *From Here to Eternity*, by James Jones, are used by permission of Charles Scribner's Sons (New York). Wm Collins Sons & Co. Ltd and the Columbia Picture Corporation have also concurred in this permission.

Photograph by Michael Boys

THE BRIDE AND THE BACHELOR

ACT I

SCENE I

SCENE—*The lounge hall of the Kilpatricks' house in St John's Wood, London. About 8 p.m. on an October evening.*

A staircase runs up the wall L *to a landing and balcony running the full width of the room to an archway up* R *leading to the bedrooms. Halfway up the staircase, in the wall* L, *are two alcoved windows. Immediately under the upstairs archway, there is a similar archway leading to the front door, kitchen, etc. French windows,* C *of the back wall, give on to a terrace and the garden beyond. The fireplace is* R *with a door below it giving access to the dining-room. The house is normal enough in design, but its furnishings and decorations are inclined to the bizarre. The furniture belongs to no particular period or nation, but appears to have been culled from the four corners of the earth. Curtains of oriental design hang at the french windows. An African figure stands in each of the staircase windows, and two tribal masks adorn the staircase walls. Both above and below the downstairs arch there are built-in bookcases packed with all shapes, sizes and colours of books, relieved by African and other ornaments. To the left of the french windows there is another similar bookcase, and, below it, under the turn of the staircase, another. There is a sofa* LC *and a matching easy chair* RC. *Below the sofa is a low coffee table and behind the sofa, a narrow polished table with a telephone on it. There is a round table up* L; *an occasional table up* R; *an armchair above the fireplace, and a fur-covered stool down* R. *At night the room is lit by wall-brackets over the mantelpiece, down* L *and at the left end of the balcony and by table-lamps up* L *and up* R. *There are switches down* L, *and up* R, *below the downstairs arch.*

(*See the Ground Plan and Photograph of the Scene*)

When the CURTAIN *rises, the lights are on and the window curtains are closed.* BARBARA KILPATRICK, *aged about sixteen, is curled up on the sofa, reading from a book on its right arm, and holding the telephone receiver to one ear. She is reading aloud from the book to an unseen listener.* BARBARA *is a typical teenager, in cotton sweater and jeans.*

BARBARA (*into the telephone*) I say, Jennifer.
GIRL'S VOICE (*off; through the telephone*) Yes?
BARBARA. Listen to this. (*She reads sensuously*) "After he was gone she went back in the bedroom."
GIRL'S VOICE. Ooooh!
BARBARA. "She put her hands down at her sides——"

GIRL'S VOICE. Ooooh!
BARBARA. "—and forced herself to relax them. She made herself breathe deeply——"

(*The doorbell rings off and is followed by a rat-a-tat-tat on the front door*)

ISABEL (*off upstairs; calling*) Blodwen! The door!
BARBARA. "—but the nerves inside her muscles went on fluttering frantically."

(MISS BOWDEN *enters up* R. *She is a capable business-woman aged about forty, dressed in a neat suit and hat. In addition to her handbag and umbrella, she carries a large dress box. She stands above the easy chair* RC)

" 'You've borne his heir for him,' she told herself. 'Who can say your life is fruitless? You've been a mother, haven't you?' "
MISS BOWDEN. Excuse me, love.

(BARBARA *drops the receiver behind the cushion*)

You're not—no, of course, you're not—the bride?
BARBARA. Why "of course"?
MISS BOWDEN. Look, I've brought the gown. (*She moves to* R *of the sofa*)
BARBARA. In Siam they marry at twelve and a half.
MISS BOWDEN. The wedding gown, for tomorrow.
BARBARA. Whereas we have to sit around and sublimate till we're practically senile.
MISS BOWDEN. I'll just put it here, love. (*She puts the box on the floor, partly under the table above the sofa, and turns towards the archway up* R, *as if to go. As she turns, her eye catches the framed photograph of Serena, which is on the downstage end of the mantelpiece*)
BARBARA. Don't you find Western civilization hopelessly primitive? (*She picks up a half-eaten apple from the coffee table*)
MISS BOWDEN (*crossing above the easy chair to the mantelpiece and gazing intently at the photograph*) That must be—it *is* the bride, isn't it?
BARBARA (*giving up*) Oh, well. Yes, that's Serena.
MISS BOWDEN. My, she's a beauty!
BARBARA. Beauty isn't everything.
MISS BOWDEN (*rooted*) My!
BARBARA. Did you know the Persian New Year begins on March the twenty-first?
MISS BOWDEN (*still gazing*) Oh, she's lovely.
BARBARA. Or that a pollard is an ox without horns?
MISS BOWDEN. It must be a grand thing—to be wed.
BARBARA. I wouldn't know. I'm a spinster. (*She bites into the apple*)

(MISS BOWDEN *moves above the easy chair*)

Haven't you ever?

MISS BOWDEN (*cheerfully*) Me? I'm a spinster, too. (*She laughs*) Well, I'll be here about ten tomorrow morning—to see her into it. Good night, love.

(MISS BOWDEN *exits up* R)

BARBARA (*calling*) Good night. (*She picks up the receiver. Into the telephone*) Jennifer, are you still there?

GIRL'S VOICE (*off; through the telephone; frenzied*) Why don't you go on, you ass?

BARBARA. I couldn't, you idiot, there was somebody here.

GIRL'S VOICE. Well, go on now.

BARBARA. O.K. (*She reads in a sensuous voice*) "Private Prewitt looked at the woman beside him. In the deep curve of her hip and the . . ."

GIRL'S VOICE. Lip?

BARBARA. No, not lip, you ass, hip. Hip, hip . .

(ISABEL KILPATRICK *enters by the upstairs archway. She is a young and fascinating fifty. In her hand she holds a scimitar*)

ISABEL (*flourishing the scimitar*) Hooray!

(BARBARA *drops the receiver behind the cushion*)

(*She comes down the stairs*) I simply can't get this into Serena's going-away bag. Such a charming present and just the thing for a honeymoon, but the shape's impossible. (*She prods Barbara's posterior with the point of the blade*) What are you up to? (*She puts the scimitar on the back of the sofa, and picks up two registered envelopes from the table above the sofa*)

BARBARA (*absorbed in the book*) Homework.

ISABEL (*crossing above the easy chair to the fireplace*) I thought I heard voices.

GIRL'S VOICE (*from the buried receiver*) Hullo—well, go on. Hullo, Babs.

BARBARA (*loudly; overlapping the voice*) I study better by reading aloud.

ISABEL (*putting the envelopes on the mantelpiece; pleasantly*) Don't shout, dear. What is it, tonight?

BARBARA. General knowledge.

ISABEL. Splendid. (*She crosses below the easy chair to* C) We can't have too much of that. And what particular aspect of general knowledge are we studying?

BARBARA. Life.

(ISABEL *suddenly seizes the book from Barbara's hands and looks at the title*)

ISABEL. "*From Here to Eternity.*"

BARBARA. In the raw.

ISABEL. And tomorrow you're to be Maid of Honour. Is nothing sacred?

BARBARA. Sex will out. We might as well face it.

ISABEL. There's a difference between facing it and rushing at it like a bull at a gate.

BARBARA. A girl's got to move with the times.

ISABEL. I took you to the movie, what more do you want?

(BARBARA *rises, moves round* L *of the sofa and looks at the presents on the table above it*)

BARBARA. They left out some of the best bits.

ISABEL (*moving below the easy chair* RC *and looking at the book*) They can't have. All those wide screens . . .

GIRL'S VOICE (*from the receiver; impatiently*) Why don't you go on? Hey, Barbara . . .

(ISABEL *hears the voice, and moves swiftly to* R *of the sofa.* BARBARA *simultaneously runs to the left end of the sofa. They both make a grab for the receiver, but* ISABEL *gets there first, picks it up and puts the book on the right arm of the sofa.* BARBARA *sits on the sofa at the left end, looking up at Isabel*)

For Pete's sake go on about Private Prewitt, you're driving me crazy.

ISABEL (*into the telephone*) We will not go on about Private Prewitt, Jennifer Soames. (*She slams the receiver down on its base*) Wretched child, she ought to be psycho-analysed. (*She crosses to the table up* L *and collects a sherry decanter and a bottle of Empire Sherry. To Barbara*) And that goes for you, too. (*She puts the decanter and bottle on the table above the sofa*)

BARBARA. I was broadening my mind.

ISABEL. Your mind needs about as much broadening as the *Encyclopaedia Britannica*. (*She moves to the table up* L, *collects a decanting funnel, and places it in the neck of the decanter*)

BARBARA. Anyone would think you wanted me to fail Higher Cert.

(ISABEL *removes the tinfoil cap from the sherry bottle, removes the cork and pours the sherry through the funnel into the decanter*)

ISABEL. So far as I'm aware, an extensive knowledge of the habits of the American Army is not essential to the acquiring of a Higher Certificate in these islands.

BARBARA. I was getting some tips for Serena in handling Joe.

ISABEL. Serena is quite capable of handling a husband without your assistance. And, in any case, Joseph is not in the Army. (*She continues decanting*)

BARBARA. He's an American.

ISABEL (*putting the sherry bottle down*) Yes, well, we can't have everything. (*She sees the dress box protruding from under the table, and*

SCENE I THE BRIDE AND THE BACHELOR 5

pulls it out) What's this? (*She reads the label.*) Barlow and Morrison's? Ah, the wedding dress—at last. (*She calls up over her right shoulder*) Serena!

(*The telephone rings.* BARBARA *leans across and lifts the receiver*) If that's Jennifer Soames again . . .
BARBARA (*into the telephone*) Hullo? . . .
MALE VOICE (*off; through the telephone*) Good evening. Is that the mother of the bride?
BARBARA. This is the bride's mother. What is your problem?

(ISABEL *finishes decanting*)

MALE VOICE. Nuptials here, madam. In view of your husband's position, would you care for red, white and blue streamers, or conventional white?

(ISABEL, *during the following speeches, returns the sherry bottle and funnel to the table up* L)

BARBARA (*to Isabel*) Nuptials, about the cars for tomorrow. Do we want just white ribbon on the bonnets, or would we like red, white and blue in honour of father?
ISABEL (*turning*) In honour of father? (*She moves to the table above the sofa*) Why?
BARBARA (*into the telephone*) Why?
MALE VOICE. We understood he was attached to the B.C.C.
BARBARA (*to Isabel*) They say they thought he worked for the British Culture Council.
ISABEL. Well, of course he works for the Culture Council, but that's the last thing one wants to . . . Here, give it to me. (*She takes the receiver from Barbara. Into the telephone*) Hullo, Nuptials. This is Mrs Kilpatrick.
MALE VOICE. Oh, good evening, madam. We were wondering . . .
ISABEL. No, we prefer to keep it dark.
MALE VOICE (*taken aback*) Dark ribbon?
ISABEL. No, not the ribbon. My husband.
MALE VOICE. Just as you wish. The cars will be there at ten-thirty exactly.
ISABEL. Splendid. Good-bye. (*She replaces the receiver*) Just look at all these presents—and not one of them even opened.
BARBARA. Mother.
ISABEL. Well, if she won't I must. We shall never get straight. (*She looks at the two boxes on the table above the sofa, picks up a pair of scissors and cuts the string of the top box*)
BARBARA (*rising and perching herself on the left arm of the sofa*) Mother, what do they do?
ISABEL (*prising up the lid of the box with the scissors; abstracted*) What do who do?
BARBARA. I mean, what are they *for*?

ISABEL. What are what for?

BARBARA. The British Culture Council.

ISABEL. Don't bother me now, dear. (*She takes out the top layer of straw packing*) Everyone knows what the Culture Council are for. (*She lifts out a very peculiar piece of pottery and holds it up for inspection*) Now, what do you suppose that's meant to be? (*She reads from the card tied to the pottery*) "May Allah bless the cultivated bride." Oh, it's from dear Sheik Gluk. (*She crosses to the fireplace*) How sweet of him. (*She reads*) "P.S. Please tell distinguished daddy I have finished the Birds and am halfway through the Frogs." (*She puts the pottery on the downstage end of the mantelpiece*) It sounds indigestible—(*she turns and crosses to the table above the sofa*) but I suppose it's all right.

BARBARA. He means Aristophanes.

ISABEL (*putting the first box under the table above the sofa and cutting the string of the second box*) Now, what have we here? Isn't it fun opening other people's presents? (*She opens the lid and takes out the top layer of packing*) Oh, isn't that sweet! (*She lifts out the present*) A skull. (*She reads the card*) "Felicitations to Daughter of Literary Adviser from M'Bonga-Bonga Tribe. Please also convey loyal greetings to T. S. Eliot." (*She crosses to* R) How thoughtful.

BARBARA. You know, sometimes the kids at school ask me about father.

ISABEL (*looking round for somewhere to place the skull*) Sweet things. (*She tries putting the skull on the mantelpiece, but as it is cluttered with presents, invitation cards and various ornaments, there is no room. She tries the bookcase, but again there is no room, and finally she moves down* R *and places the skull on the stool below the fireplace*)

BARBARA. When I tell them he works for the Council, they either look puzzled or start to laugh hysterically.

ISABEL. Then they're a lot of bad-mannered, ignorant little girls. The Culture Council is a splendid institution. (*She is not happy with the skull on the stool, picks it up again, moves up* RC, *then puts it on the back of the easy chair, with the skull's face upstage*).

BARBARA. Why?

ISABEL (*regarding the skull with distaste*) Why? Because it—it shows the flag and—and spreads the good word, that's why.

BARBARA. What word?

ISABEL. It takes British culture to the people of the world—(*she turns the skull to face the audience*) and vice versa.

BARBARA. Such as what?

ISABEL. Don't bother me now, dear. (*She moves above the easy chair*) I'm busy.

BARBARA. Such as what?

ISABEL (*desperately*) Such as teaching Elizabethan madrigals to Burmese laundry-women and explaining Benjamin Britten to the natives of Nigeria. And it doesn't cost a penny over three million a year.

SCENE I   THE BRIDE AND THE BACHELOR   7

BARBARA (*rising*) That ain't hay! (*She sits* C *of the sofa*)
ISABEL. Don't be vulgar! We can't pay too much for culture. (*She sees the skull again, picks it up and tosses it into the waste-paper basket full of gift wrappings,* R *of the sofa*) I'm fed up with that, anyway. (*She moves below the easy chair*) Your father says that if the Whirling Dervishes had only been taught the *Ode to a Grecian Urn* when they were tiny, they would probably never have taken up whirling at all and then Lord Kitchener wouldn't have been assassinated at Khartoum.
BARBARA. He wasn't. It was General Gordon.
ISABEL. Nonsense! Gordon led the Charge of the Light Brigade.

(SERENA KILPATRICK *appears through the upstairs archway and moves along the balcony towards the head of the stairs. She is a lovely girl of twenty-one. She appears preoccupied*)

(*She moves up* L *of the easy chair*) Oh, there you are, Serena. Darling, it's arrived.
SERENA. What has? (*She moves down the stairs*)
ISABEL. The wedding dress. Isn't it exciting?

(SERENA *stops halfway down the stairs*)

Well, say something.
SERENA. Oh. (*She proceeds to the bottom of the stairs, picks up the duffel coat draped over the newel post, and puts it on*)
ISABEL. Serena, your father sold his three per cent Gas Shares to pay for it. Is that the best you can do?

(SERENA *crosses to the french windows*)

Serena!
SERENA. I'm going for a walk, Mummy.
ISABEL. *Another* walk? How very peculiar. Why?
SERENA. I like walking.
ISABEL. Until a week ago it was all we could do to get you to set one foot in front of the other.
SERENA. People change.
ISABEL (*crossing and standing above the sofa*) Stop talking nonsense and come and open these presents.
SERENA (*moving to the pillar up* RC) There's no hurry.
ISABEL. No hurry? You *are* marrying Joseph Washington Tilney first thing in the morning?
SERENA. I suppose so.
ISABEL. Well, come along, then, we're snowed under. (*She picks up the scissors*)
BARBARA. Three more parcels have arrived.
SERENA. *Three!*
ISABEL. Yes, three. Isn't it fun?
SERENA (*moving* C; *in a panic*) It's two too many. *It's two too many.*

(SERENA *rushes out by the french windows*)

ISABEL (*bewildered*) Two too many? What in the world's the matter with her?
BARBARA. Maybe she wants one last breath of freedom before being committed.
ISABEL (*dropping the scissors on to the table*) It's Holy Wedlock she's entering, dear, not an institution.

(BLODWEN MORGAN-JONES *enters up* R. *She is of indeterminate age, the general factotum of the household. Her solemn manner is relieved on occasion by a smile or native eloquence. At the moment she is sunk in gloom. She carries a book tucked under her arm*)

BLODWEN (*moving to* R *of Isabel*) Pardon the intrusion . . .
ISABEL. Yes, Blodwen, what is it? (*She picks up the waste-paper basket and puts it* R *of the table up* L)
BLODWEN. Sorry I am to be saying it, but desirous I am of giving the notice.
ISABEL. Notice!
BLODWEN. All this happiness in the home. I do not think I can endure it.
ISABEL. Now what's the matter with you?
BARBARA. Psycho-sexual frustration.
ISABEL. Barbara, go to your room.
BARBARA. I haven't had supper.
ISABEL. We're not having supper tonight, it's sandwiches. Take two with you and go straight to bed.

(BARBARA *picks up the plate of sandwiches from the coffee table, takes two sandwiches, then reaches over the back of the sofa and puts the plate on top of the skull box on the table above the sofa*)

BARBARA. And read?
ISABEL. If you must.

(BARBARA *grabs "From Here to Eternity"*)

Barbara!
BARBARA. You can have a bash when I've finished.
ISABEL. I have no intention of having a bash.
BARBARA (*reluctantly dropping the book on to the sofa*) There's nothing else. (*She rises and moves slowly up the stairs*)
ISABEL. Don't be absurd! What's that one Aunt Alicia gave you for having your wisdom tooth out?
BARBARA (*halting halfway up the stairs; derisively*) *Hockeystick Hilda comes home for the Hols.*
ISABEL. Yes, well, you pop in between the sheets with Hockeystick Hilda.
BARBARA (*proceeding up the stairs*) Really, Mother! Is nothing sacred?

(BARBARA *exits by the upstairs arch*)

ISABEL (*sitting on the right arm of the sofa*) Now, what's all this about giving notice?
BLODWEN (*standing up* L *of the easy chair*) Regretful I am, but desirous I am.
ISABEL. Yes, but untimely it is, and reluctant we are.
BLODWEN (*with an admiring smile*) My, but you have the Welsh lovely.
ISABEL (*pleased*) Oh, do you think so?
BLODWEN. The music is there and the lilt. You don't often run into the lilt and the music this side of the valley.
ISABEL. Well, that's only to be expected, isn't it?
BLODWEN. Nothing in life is to be expected—bar the leaving of it. Santayana said that, and good luck to him. Which reminds me—(*she hands the book to Isabel*) return I do herewith the *Letters of George Bernard Shaw* to Miss Ellen Terry and vice versa.
ISABEL. They're rather fun, aren't they? (*She rises, moves to the bookcase up* LC *and puts the book on the shelf*)
BLODWEN. Fun? I'm disgusted! (*She moves round the easy chair and stands above it*)
ISABEL. Oh, dear. I'm so sorry. (*She turns and moves down a step*) What happened?
BLODWEN. Nothing. That's why I'm disgusted.
ISABEL (*moving and sitting on the right arm of the sofa*) I'm not sure that I follow.
BLODWEN. Only one proper meeting they had in the whole of their lives—(*she sits on the left arm of the easy chair*) and them loving each other like one o'clock.
ISABEL. Ah, but theirs was a very special relationship. They sublimated—through the post, as it were.
BLODWEN (*rising; firmly*) All against sublimation we are in the Valley. All for action we are. And what I say is, if love is just letters and letters is love, why dammit you've had it, well, isn't it? (*She moves up* R) Which reminds me. (*She turns*) Good-bye now.
ISABEL (*rising; distracted*) No, wait! Blodwen! You can't possibly leave now. What *has* happened?
BLODWEN (*moving below the easy chair*) Thinkin' I am of the wedding tomorrow, and Miss Serena, the Lord love her, taking a man to herself, it comes to me forceful, me, Blodwen Morgan-Jones, the unmarried person, that I should be devoting myself to securing a man for myself, isn't it?
ISABEL (*moving to* L *of Blodwen*) Well, yes, of course, everyone should have a man in their lives. But couldn't you possibly combine business with pleasure?
BLODWEN. I do not take your meaning.
ISABEL. Well, there's the milkman—and the postman—and the greengrocer's boy . . .
BLODWEN (*turning* R; *stubbornly*) Regretful I am, but desirous I am.

ISABEL (*circling below, then above the sofa to* C) But you've no right to be desirous at a time like this! So much happiness in the air——

BLODWEN (*turning away*) Too much happiness can be very depressing.

ISABEL (*clutching at straws*) It won't last. It never does. Surely that's a comfort. (*She moves between the sofa and the easy chair*) Try and look on the black side. And we'll do our utmost to control our natural high spirits. I'm sure if we concentrate we can manage to be miserable for at least part of the day.

BLODWEN (*moving* R *of the easy chair towards the arch up* R) It would be appreciated.

(*The telephone rings.* BLODWEN *stops and turns*)

ISABEL. Bother! (*She lifts the telephone receiver. Into the telephone*) Hallo?

(*The sound of jazz music comes over the telephone*)

JOE (*off; through the telephone; loudly*) Hi, there, Momsy.

ISABEL. Oh, hallo, Joe darling. Just a minute. (*She picks up "From Here to Eternity"*) Blodwen, take this. (*She hands the book to Blodwen*) It may do something for you. (*Into the telephone*) I'm sorry, Joe.

(BLODWEN *studies the book*)

JOE (*off*) Could I have a word with sugar-plum?
ISABEL. Sugar-plum's out, dear.
JOE (*off*) No kidding?
ISABEL. Believe it or not, she's roaming around somewhere, breathing her last breath——
JOE (*off*) Huh?
ISABEL. —of freedom. You know what girls are.
BLODWEN (*suddenly*) Oooh! (*She moves to* R *of Isabel and taps her arm*)
ISABEL (*into the telephone*) Hang on. Trouble.
BLODWEN (*showing the book to Isabel and reading*) "Private Prewitt looked at the woman beside him . . ." They would like this in the Valley.

(BLODWEN, *reading hard, exits up* R. ISABEL *sighs with relief*)

JOE (*off*) Say, listen, Momsy, tell Sugar . . .
ISABEL. Joe, you sound very loud and penetrating—where are you?
JOE (*off*) Round the corner with Simon and Scotty.
ISABEL. With Simon and Scotty. Ah. (*She becomes aware of the musical background*) There seems to be some sort of hullabaloo going on, I can't quite . . .
JOE (*off*) It's a stag party. The boys are whoopin' it up.

ISABEL (*cautiously*) A stag party? Oh.
JOE (*off*) We're gonna pass it around a little.
ISABEL. Just what is it you're planning to pass, Joseph?
JOE (*off*) Now, Momsy...
ISABEL. Well, I'm sure you'd all feel much better tomorrow if you stuck to Ovaltine. We don't want any hiccupping during the responses.
JOE (*off*) Momsy!
ISABEL. Well, you three stags be careful.
JOE (*off; laughing*) I'm with you, Momsy. Give Sugar a smooch for me. And Simon, and Scotty.
ISABEL. Three smooches. Right.

(*Sounds of arrival are heard off up* R)

Wait. Here she is now.
JASON (*off up* R) Good evening, Blodwen.
BLODWEN (*off up* R) Good evening, Mr Kilpatrick, sir.
ISABEL (*into the telephone*) No, it's only Jason. See you in church. Good-bye, Joe. (*She replaces the receiver*)
JASON (*off; overlapping Isabel's farewells*) All right, Blodwen. I can manage it.

(JASON KILPATRICK *enters sideways up* R, *struggling with an Egyptian Mummy case as big as himself. He is a mild-mannered man with glasses, dressed in traditional "City" garb*)

Hallo, my dear. (*He moves to Isabel, manœuvring the Mummy case round in front of him as he comes*)

(ISABEL *goes to kiss Jason and nearly kisses the Mummy case instead*)

ISABEL. Jason! This is no time for learning the cello.
JASON (*breathless*) My dear, it's a Mummy case. "From the Sons of the Daughters of the Nile to the Daughter of the Son of Kilpatrick." A most generous gift. I do hope Serena will like it.
ISABEL. I'm sure she'll adore it. (*She kisses Jason round the front of the Mummy case*) She's been wanting one of those for years. (*She picks up the decanter from the table above the sofa, puts it on the coffee table, then moves up* L *of the sofa to the table up* L, *collects two sherry glasses and puts them with the decanter*)
JASON. My goodness, my wind isn't what it was. (*He moves the Mummy case up* R) I had quite a tussle with that in the Tube. (*He hangs his bowler hat outside the arch up* R *and gives the Mummy case a pat*)
ISABEL. Have a sandwich. (*She transfers the sandwiches from the table above the sofa to the coffee table*)
JASON (*moving down* C) Thanks, I don't think I will, dear, not just before supper.

ISABEL (*sitting on the sofa at the left end*) This is supper. (*She pours two glasses of sherry*)

JASON. Oh. Pity. (*He sits* R *of Isabel on the sofa and takes a sandwich*) Quite a day it's been, one way and another. What with Proudfoot's opening lecture for the Zurutis.

ISABEL. You don't mean to tell me those cannibals have actually arrived?

JASON. Rather! They got in from the Gold Coast this morning. Proudfoot's a most effective speaker. They simply ate him up.

ISABEL. What was he lecturing them about?

JASON. The place of the French horn in London music of the eighteenth century.

ISABEL. Then he got what was coming to him.

JASON. Oh, and I say, here's a treat. The Zurutis have promised to perform their ceremonial wedding dance on our front lawn afterwards. Weather permitting.

ISABEL. I shall pray hard for rain. (*She tries a sandwich, returns it in disgust to the plate, takes a cigarette and lighter from her bag, but does not yet smoke, but puts the case and lighter on the coffee table*)

JASON. Oh, but it's a splendid thing. Wild and primitive—a great whirling and rushing about in abandonment. (*He rises and moves* C) At the end of the dance they lie flat on their backs and make a hundred and fifty kahootis—or kicks—with their legs crossed. And if you think that's easy, you try it. (*He moves* R)

ISABEL. I don't think I'll bother.

JASON (*moving to the fireplace*) Hallo, more presents?

ISABEL (*indicating the piece of pottery on the mantelpiece*) That extraordinary-looking object is from Sheik Gluk.

JASON (*examining it*) Ah yes. A ceremonial wattle-bottle.

ISABEL. He's having a high old time with the birds and the bees or something.

JASON. Good for Gluk. He was one of my earliest successes. I started him off on *Alice in Wonderland*, and do you know, within a week—(*he moves above the easy chair*) he'd worked his way up to *Lady Chatterley's Lover*.

ISABEL. Remarkable.

JASON. One doesn't want to sound boastful or over-weening, but little things like that do rather warm the heart and encourage one to go on. As Proudfoot says:

"Cricket and Soccer and so forth
Are all very well in their way,
But it's culture that keeps the old country
On top—and so that's why we say
Anyone here for Culture?
Cheerio! Tally-ho! Hi-de-hay."

Very moving. (*He moves* R) Is Serena upstairs? (*He crosses to* C)

ISABEL. No. She's out walking. It's her fourth walk in three days. I'm quite worried about it.

JASON (*sitting R of Isabel on the sofa*) Are you, dear? Why?
ISABEL. You know she always takes taxis. All this footwork is most unnatural. It's nerves, of course. (*Worried*) You can see from her eyes she's not sleeping properly. I hope she's going to be all right. I do so want her to be happy, darling. I couldn't bear it if . . . Perhaps I should have a little talk to her, last thing.
JASON. What about, dear?
ISABEL. Don't be silly, dear.
JASON. You mean, persuade her to take the occasional bus? Good idea.
ISABEL. Sometimes a cosy little chat makes all the difference at a time like this. I remember the night before I was to marry you, naturally I was feeling rather depressed, and then mother came in and had a little talk.
JASON. Did it help?
ISABEL. By the time she was through, I was fit to be certified.
JASON (*vaguely*) Oh, well. Better luck next time.
ISABEL. I *beg* your pardon?

(*The sound of African drumming is heard off, gradually increasing in volume.*

BARBARA *runs on by the upstairs arch. She is in pyjamas and dressing-gown*)

BARBARA (*moving C of the balcony; excitedly*) Mother! A couple of natives are coming up the drive.
ISABEL. What sort of natives?
BARBARA. Well, one's got a spear, and the other a sort of blow-pipe thing with feathers.

(JASON *rises, moves to the french windows and looks out*)

ISABEL (*rising*) My God, the cannibals!
JASON (*moving down C*) My dear, you really must not refer to them as cannibals. The Zurutis are a proud and ancient race . . .
ISABEL (*moving to L of the sofa*) Then what do they want with the Kilpatricks at this time of night?
BARBARA. Dinner, I should think. They look hungry.

(ISABEL *continues up L, looks out of the windows, then turns and moves down L*)

JASON. Oh, I hardly think so. We arranged for them to have shepherd's pie at Swiss Cottage. Or was it cottage pie at Shepherd's Bush?

(*There is a loud knocking off up R.* BLODWEN, *off up R, shrieks*)

(*He moves up C and looks off R*) Steady, Blodwen!
ISABEL (*crossing to L of Jason*) All right, Blodwen, we'll answer it. (*Urgently*) Barbara, go straight to your room, lock the door and bolt it.

JASON. My dear, I assure you . . .
ISABEL. Jason, stand at the door and—what's the word . . .?
BARBARA (*who has not budged from the balcony*) Palaver.
ISABEL. That's right—palaver.
BARBARA. Mammy palaver, actually.
ISABEL. Mammy will certainly not palaver. Daddy will palaver —but Mammy will be right behind him.

(*There is more knocking on the front door*)

(*She pushes Jason off up* R) Don't be afraid. At the first sign of attack I shall dial nine-nine-nine.

(JASON *exits up* R. *His voice is heard over the drumming, greeting the Zuruti tribesmen.* BARBARA *comes down the stairs*)

(*She circles the easy chair and stands down* R) I do wish your father would look a little less like a Civil Servant and more like Gregory Peck in *King Solomon's Mines*.

BARBARA (*perching on the left arm of the sofa*) It wasn't Peck. It was Granger.
ISABEL. I don't care if it was Lassie!

(BLODWEN *runs on up* R, *crosses to* R *of the easy chair, then crosses below the sofa to the stairs*)

BLODWEN (*in a frenzy*) There is a great big black man standing at the front door, and a mighty host from Africa lined up behind him—(*she goes up the stairs*)

(BARBARA *rises and moves to the french windows.* ISABEL *circles the sofa, following Blodwen*)

—knives, and spears and drums, and the Lord have mercy on all poor sinners.

(BLODWEN *exits by the upstairs archway*)

JASON (*off*) Bakkaliki!

(*The African voices cease*)

ISABEL (*grabbing the scimitar and charging towards the arch up* R) Charge! (*She brandishes the scimitar*)

(*The drums stop.*
JASON *enters up* R. *He carries an African spear, a volume of parchment, a wooden bowl, a brass nose-ring and is wearing a beribboned flower garland. He is checked abruptly by the scimitar*)

JASON. It's only me, dear.
ISABEL (*putting the scimitar on the back of the sofa*) Jason! (*She moves down* R *of the sofa*) You look like a Beefeater at the Chelsea Flower Show.

JASON (*moving down* C) My dear, these are wedding presents.
ISABEL. Wedding presents?
JASON. It's an old Zuruti custom to honour the bride and her groom and her family on the eve of the wedding. Now, what have we here? "The Spear of Joy", for the groom. (*He holds out the spear*)

(ISABEL *takes the spear in both hands and holds it* L *of herself, looking at the blade*)

Symbolic, of course. (*He bends* R *as if to put the bowl and ring on the easy chair*)

ISABEL. I should hope so. (*Examining the spear she tilts the shaft to* R, *and catches the bending Jason in the buttocks*)

JASON (*straightening up*) I say! Steady! (*He takes the spear from Isabel and bends* R *again, to put the bowl on the easy chair, and tilts the spear to* L)

ISABEL (*bending over the right end of the coffee table and taking a cigarette from her case*) Babs, see if they've gone.

(*The tilting spear catches* ISABEL'S *hindquarters*)

(*To Jason*) Don't do that, dear. I don't like it.
JASON. I *beg* your pardon, dear.

(BARBARA *moves to* R *of Jason, takes the spear from him and leans it against the wall below the door down* R)

BARBARA. It's O.K. They're getting into a taxi.

(ISABEL *sits on the sofa, at the left end*)

JASON. What next? "The Brass Ring of Bereavement", for the girl's mother. (*He hands what looks like a large curtain ring to Isabel*)

(ISABEL *tries the ring on her left hand, but it is too big*)

It's worn through the nose, dear.

(ISABEL *puts the ring on her nose*)

"The Garland of Anticipation" for the bridal attendant. (*He hangs the garland around Barbara's neck*)

BARBARA. Oh, lovely! (*She circles round, displaying the adornment, then sits on the right arm of the easy chair*)

JASON. "The Book of Provocative Thought" for the father of the bride.

(ISABEL *picks up her lighter and attempts to light the cigarette through the nose ring. After a couple of puffs she tries to drink some sherry, but again the ring gets in the way*)

(*He sits on the left arm of the easy chair*) Ah, our old friend Boccachio's *Decameron* in Zuruti. And for the bride herself, the "Denkol Palamink" or "Little Bowl of Faith". (*He rises, moves to Isabel, hands her the bowl, then sits* R *of her on the sofa*)

(ISABEL *removes the nose ring and puts it on the coffee table*)

There's a charming legend about the "Denkol Palamink". I don't know if you've heard it. Stop me if you have.

ISABEL. Stop!

JASON. Should the bride-to-be require help from above, the Bowl is held to the midnight moon by her Dim-Dim . . .

ISABEL. Her what-what?

JASON (*explaining*) Witch doctor, who chants the wisdom of the ages inscribed round the rim, and the invocation is answered.

ISABEL (*putting the bowl on the coffee table*) By whom?

(SERENA *enters up* R *and crosses to* C. *She removes her coat and puts it on the back of the easy chair*)

Serena!

JASON. Ah, there you are, my dear. Try an omnibus once in a while. Your mother would appreciate it. (*He rises, takes the book with him, crosses, sits on the stool below the fireplace, and reads*)

ISABEL. Serena, where *have* you been?

SERENA. Has anyone seen *The Doors of Perception*? (*She looks in the bookcase up* R)

ISABEL. I do wish you wouldn't take off like that. At a time like this one likes to keep track.

BARBARA (*rising and pirouetting to the foot of the stairs*) I shall wear this to the church tomorrow. I may wear it indefinitely.

(SERENA *crosses and looks under the right sofa cushion*)

ISABEL. Serena, are you receiving me?

SERENA (*kissing the top of Isabel's head*) Sorry, Mummy. Not really. (*She crosses to the bookcase up* RC *and looks in it*)

BARBARA (*on the second stair*) "The Garland of Anticipation."

JASON (*rising*) Of course, that's a free translation, Babs, dear. *Baranta Lagol* means literally, "One-day-me-too".

BARBARA (*deeply impressed*) "One-day-me-too." What a beautiful thought.

(JASON *moves to the table lamp up* R, *switches it on, then sits in the armchair up* R, *and reads*)

SERENA (*moving down* C) It's only a little book. About sixty pages. (*She looks under the cushion of the easy chair*)

ISABEL. Serena, are you feeling quite well?

SERENA (*crossing and looking in the bookcase up* L) As a matter of fact, I think I'm going to be sick.

ISABEL. That's because you've had nothing to eat. Come along, have a sandwich.

BARBARA. Ugh! I wouldn't if I were you.

ISABEL. Barbara!

BARBARA. Well, she said she felt sick already.

ISABEL. Barbara, go to your room——

BARBARA } (*together*) —and stay there.
ISABEL

BARBARA. Don't say I didn't warn you. (*She goes up the stairs, singing and circling as she goes*) One, two, three o'clock, four o'clock rock; five, six, seven o'clock, eight o'clock rock . . .

(BARBARA *exits by the upstairs arch.* SERENA *finds the book in the bookcase up* L)

ISABEL. Darling, where have you been?

SERENA (*moving* C; *dreamily*) Just walking. I stood on a hill and looked at the dome of heaven, Mummy. The stars fixed in their courses—the moon, so still and clear and sure of itself—and I felt a sudden, strange affinity with the universe. As if—as if by stretching up my hand I could touch eternity. And then I thought of Aldous Huxley, and I knew he was right. (*She sits* R *of Isabel on the sofa*)

ISABEL. Right about what?

SERENA (*opening the book*) Marriage. Listen. (*She reads*) "Embraced, the lovers desperately try to fuse their insulated ecstasies into a single self-transcendence. In vain." In vain. You see?

(ISABEL *does not see*)

Even two into one is impossible. But *three*!

ISABEL (*bewildered*) Three?

SERENA (*leaning on the right arm of the sofa*) Love is so terribly, terribly sad.

ISABEL (*severely*) Serena, have you been talking to Blodwen?

SERENA (*with an arm round Isabel*) No. Only to myself.

(JASON, *deep in his book, gives a sudden roar of laughter*)

Sad—and complicated. Like life, when you come to think about it.

ISABEL. Then don't think about it. Just live it.

SERENA. I can't. I'm too sensitive.

(JASON *hoots with laughter.* ISABEL *takes the book from Serena, rises and crosses to Jason*)

ISABEL. One thing at least is clear to me about this household. Too many people are reading too many books. (*She snatches Jason's book, then crosses and puts both books on the table above the sofa*)

JASON. Yes, dear.

ISABEL (*moving to* R *of the sofa; to Serena*) I shall ask Joe to keep a strict eye on your library.

SERENA. We probably won't be able to afford one.

ISABEL. So much the better. Now try and get your mind off

Mr Huxley and on to something sober and sensible. (*She sits on the right arm of the sofa*)

JASON. I heard an odd thing today. Do you know the average man spends three thousand four hundred hours of his life shaving and having his hair cut?

ISABEL (*to Serena*) There you are. There's a nice clean thought to go to bed with. (*She rises, then picks up the dress box*) Up you go now——

(SERENA *rises*)

—and take this with you.

SERENA. What is it? (*She realizes. Blankly*) Oh. (*She takes the box from Isabel and moves down* L)

JASON (*taking out a pocketbook and pencil*) Three thousand four hundred hours just cutting off bits of hair.

(SERENA *goes slowly up the stairs*)

ISABEL (*moving to the coffee table*) Good night, my darling. (*She picks up the decanter*) Pleasant dreams.

SERENA (*at once; trembling*) Don't. Don't say that!

ISABEL (*moving to the table up* L) Don't be silly, dear. I've been saying it every night for twenty-one years. (*She puts the decanter on the table up* L) Now go straight to sleep—(*she moves to the coffee table*) and remember, there's nothing to worry about. (*She picks up the sherry glasses*) I've packed your going-away bag, to save time in the morning. (*She moves to the table up* L) I wasn't sure what you wanted, so I put in three of everything. (*She puts the glasses on the table up* L)

SERENA (*leaning over the balcony; violently*) No! No, Mummy, no! *Not three!* Please, please, *please*—not *three*!

(SERENA *drops the dress box on the balcony and rushes wildly out by the upstairs archway*)

ISABEL (*going up the stairs and looking after Serena*) You know, that child's rapidly becoming abnormal. If she weren't your *adopted* daughter—(*she leans over the right end of the balcony*) we'd know where she gets it. But a *foster* father can't hand on his hormones—or can he? (*She pauses*) I say, "Or can he?" Jason, don't just sit there, say something.

JASON (*stroking his chin*) Of course, with an electric razor, I fancy one could get the figure down to around three thousand two hundred and fifty . . .

(ISABEL *gives a cluck of exasperation and picks up the dress box*)

ISABEL (*calling*) Darling! Mummy's coming up to have a little chat.

ISABEL *exits by the upstairs archway as—*

the CURTAIN *falls*

SCENE 2

SCENE—*The same. Three hours later.*

When the CURTAIN *rises, the only light in the room is the moonlight which streams through the staircase windows, throwing an arc of light across the room to the fireplace, where the fire glows dimly. There is a fractional pause, then a scream comes from somewhere upstairs. Almost immediately a light goes on in the upstairs archway, and* SERENA, *in her nightgown, enters and runs along the balcony. She stops at the head of the stairs, looks wildly around, then runs down the stairs, and switches on the wall-brackets by the switches at the foot of the stairs. She crosses and drops breathless into the easy chair.* BARBARA, *in dressing-gown and pyjamas, and with the garland round her neck, enters by the upstairs archway.*

BARBARA (*over the balcony; in a loud whisper*) Okay, it's only me.

(SERENA *sits quivering and distraught*)

(*She comes down the stairs and stands down* L *of the sofa*) Another dream?
SERENA. Yes. My golden wedding!
BARBARA. To Joe?
SERENA. *And* Simon *and* Scotty!
BARBARA (*wide-eyed*) *Three* bridegrooms?
SERENA (*miserably*) Yes, three!
BARBARA. What happened?
SERENA (*rising and crossing to the sofa*) We went to the *Savoy*—and had a little dinner—and danced. (*She sits on the right arm of the sofa*)
BARBARA. What's wrong with that?
SERENA (*passionately*) Everything. I did three anniversary waltzes—one with Joe, one with Simon and one with Scotty. And—and then—(*she rises*) they stood up and sang "We've been together now for fifty years—and it don't seem a day too much."
BARBARA (*wide-eyed*) All three?
SERENA (*desperately*) In harmony!
BARBARA. Golly! And then?
SERENA. I woke up—screaming. (*She sits on the sofa at the right end*) Babs, do you think I'm going mad?
BARBARA. Yes.
SERENA. So do I. And I'm marrying Joe in the morning. (*She rises and crosses to* RC) What *am* I to do?
BARBARA. I'll make some Nescaf.
SERENA. No. It's all right. You'd better go back to bed, baby. (*She sits in the easy chair*)
BARBARA. What about you?
SERENA. I daren't.
BARBARA. You'll have to go to bed sometime.

SERENA. I may never be able to go to bed again.

BARBARA (*thoughtfully*) Gosh! Poor old Joe. (*Suddenly*) I know what. I'll read to you. (*She moves to the bookcase up* L)

SERENA (*eagerly*) Would you? Babs, you're an angel.

BARBARA. What would you like? (*She looks along the shelves*) *Three Men in a Boat?*

SERENA. That's not funny!

BARBARA. *The Three Musketeers?*

(SERENA *sits up, clutches the cushion and turns away*)

SERENA. *Don't!*

BARBARA (*picking out a book*) How's this? *First Steps in Spellbinding.* (*She moves down* C) A practical primer for beginners, by Deirdre Messiter-Jones. Okay?

SERENA (*relaxing*) Okay.

(BARBARA *lies on the sofa at the left end and opens the book*)

BARBARA (*reading*) "Chapter one. Let us begin with the magic of love."

SERENA (*rising and moving up* C) I've got a thirst like a fish.

BARBARA (*crossly*) Oh, for Pete's sake! There's some milk in the fridge. (*She puts the book on the seat of the sofa at the left end, turns over and lies along the sofa to continue reading*)

SERENA. Shan't be a sec.

(SERENA *exits up* R)

BARBARA (*absorbed; reading aloud to herself*) "In love magic, attractive scents are the current fad. Mixed carefully in a cupella or little bowl, it has been found . . ." (*Suddenly*) Golly Moses! The African bowl. (*She sits up,* C *of the sofa, picks up the bowl from the coffee table, and tries to remember Jason's instructions*) Should the bride-to-be require help—(*she looks upwards*) from above, her Dim-Dim, or witch doctor, holds this little spittoon affair to the midnight moon, and chants the wisdom of the ages—(*she looks at the bowl*) inscribed round the rim and the invocation is answered. (*She excitedly turns the bowl this way and that, then rises, moves to the french windows and opens the curtains*)

(*Moonlight floods in the french windows*)

(*Triumphantly*) A full moon. We're in business. (*She calls*) Hey, Serena! No, wait, I'll do it, I'm less contaminated. (*Standing in the french windows, she solemnly holds the bowl up to the midnight moon*)

(ISABEL *enters simultaneously by the upstairs archway. She wears a housecoat and brandishes a knobkerrie. She cannot see, or be seen by Barbara. As* BARBARA *opens her mouth to speak,* ISABEL *moves to* C *of the balcony and leans over*)

ISABEL. Don't move. If it's shepherd's pie you're after, we're clean out of stock.

(BARBARA, *startled, turns, quickly recovers, moves* C *and looks up at Isabel*)

BARBARA. Hi!
ISABEL. Barbara!
BARBARA (*circling down* C *to the down* L *corner of the sofa; rhapsodically*) What a wonderful night. Will you dig that craaazy moon?
ISABEL. Barbara Kilpatrick, do you know what time it is?
BARBARA (*lying back on the left arm of the sofa*) Just on midnight. "On such a night as this . . ."
ISABEL (*coming down the stairs*) On such a night as this, may I ask why you're bound for the garden in your Viyella?
BARBARA. If moonlight sends you, it sends you. (*She rises*) Look at Beethoven.
ISABEL (*at the foot of the stairs; brandishing the knobkerrie*) Upstairs! Up, this instant. (*She crosses below the sofa*)

(BARBARA *moves to the stairs*)

(*She indicates the garland*) And kindly remove that shrub. We're not in Honolulu.
BARBARA (*going upstairs and holding the bowl up ceremonially in front of her*) Some people have no soul.
ISABEL (*crossing to* R *of the banisters*) And give me that pot.
BARBARA (*handing the bowl over the banisters to Isabel*) Can't I take it to bed with me?
ISABEL (*crossing above the sofa to* C; *briskly*) Certainly not, you're a big girl now.
BARBARA. You're stunting my intellect.
ISABEL. If you're not up those stairs in . . .
BARBARA. But look—it's inscribed with the wisdom of the ages.
ISABEL. I'll inscribe you with the wisdom of the ages if you don't take off this second.

(BARBARA *trudges slowly up the stairs*)

Come along, quicker than that, quicker than that.

(BARBARA *exits by the upstairs archway*)

(*Scornfully*) Inscribed with the wisdom of the ages. (*She puts the knobkerrie on the floor above the sofa*)

(*A distant clock strikes midnight*)

(*She moves up* R, *switches off the wall-brackets by the switches below the arch up* R, *circles above the right end of the sofa to the french windows and holds the bowl up in the moonlight. She slowly and with difficulty picks out the inscription round the rim of the bowl*) "Quel—atranta—quel atronta—quel atronta—quel atrine." The child's raving. (*She turns and puts the bowl on the table above the sofa*) Absolutely raving.

(She continues down C, *crosses below the sofa to* L *and goes up the stairs, singing to the tune of "Clementine")* "Quel—atranta—quel—atronta —quel atronta—quel—atrine." Never—heard—such—ruddy— nonsense—Oh, my darling—Clementine.

(ISABEL *exits by the upstairs arch. The light in the upstairs archway is switched off. At once, the sound of wind is heard. The french windows open slowly of their own accord.*

SIR WILLIAM BENEDICK-BARLOW *strolls into the room by the french windows. He is a man of comfortable build, dressed in morning clothes. He sports a red carnation. The wind stops. The french windows close)*

SIR WILLIAM *(looking around him)* God bless my soul! *(He moves to the easy chair and sinks into it)*

(SERENA *enters up* R. *She carries a plate of sandwiches. She crosses to the table up* L *and switches on the lamp)*

SERENA *(turning)* Babs! *(She crosses above the easy chair to* R *of it and suddenly sees Sir William)* Oh, hallo.

SIR WILLIAM. Hallo.

SERENA. I say, are you feeling all right?

SIR WILLIAM. Yes. That is . . .

SERENA. You don't look all right. *(She offers him the plate of sandwiches)* Would you care for a sandwich?

SIR WILLIAM. I'd prefer a rather strong drink.

SERENA *(crossing to the table up* L*)* I doubt if we have anything stronger than Empire Sherry. Daddy works for the British Culture Council.

SIR WILLIAM. Oh dear.

SERENA *(putting the sandwiches on the table up* L*)* Yes, we have. It must be for tomorrow. Do you like whisky? *(She pours a stiff drink)* I think it tastes horrid. Like drinking sandpaper.

SIR WILLIAM. It's not so much the taste as—the general effect. In moments of stress, a whisky and soda has been known to have a—a becalming influence. *(He sits up, facing front)*

SERENA. In that case, I'll have one, too. *(She pours a second drink)* If ever a girl needed becalming, it's me. *(She picks up both drinks and crosses to* L *of the easy chair)* If I'm ill, it won't be the Scotch, just my mental condition. *(She hands a glass to Sir William)*

SIR WILLIAM. Mental?

SERENA. Yes, it runs in the family. *(She raises her glass)* Down the Colney Hatch.

SIR WILLIAM *(raising his glass)* Your very good health. *(He drinks and drains his glass in one gulp)*

(SERENA *drinks and grimaces)*

SERENA. Sandpaper. *(She sits on the right arm of the sofa)* Have you known Joe for long?

Scene 2   THE BRIDE AND THE BACHELOR   23

SIR WILLIAM. Joe?
SERENA. You are one of Joe's, aren't you?
SIR WILLIAM (*blankly*) One of Joe's . . .?
SERENA. Friends. You know—bride or groom.
SIR WILLIAM. No. No, I'm not one of Joe's.
SERENA. You have come for the wedding?
SIR WILLIAM. Er—yes. That is—not exactly.
SERENA. You aren't a burglar? If you're after the presents, there are some on there and the rest are in the dining-room.
SIR WILLIAM (*proffering his glass*) I wonder if I could trouble you for another whisky?
SERENA. You do absorb, don't you? (*She rises*) Promise you won't pass out on me? (*She moves to the table up* L *and picks up the whisky bottle*)
SIR WILLIAM. I won't pass out on you.

(SERENA *moves* C, *refills Sir William's glass, then her own, and puts the bottle on the coffee table*)

SERENA. Here we go again, then. (*She raises her glass*) Your very good health.
SIR WILLIAM (*raising his glass*) Down the Colney Hatch!

(*They drink*)

SERENA. Mmm. I see what you mean about that becalming business. (*She circles upstage round the right end of the sofa, then moves above the left end of it and finally comes down* L) I'm beginning to feel beautifully becalmed, as if I were sailing away on a river of candy floss.

(*The light in the upstairs archway is switched on.*
    ISABEL *storms on to the balcony by the upstairs arch*)

ISABEL. Now, look here, Barbara, once and for all . . . (*She sees Serena. Amazed*) Serena!
SERENA. Drifting along in a tiny canoe down the sensuous stream of life.
ISABEL. What in the world are you doing down there?
SERENA (*lying on the sofa with her head at the left end*) I'm floating, Mummy.
ISABEL (*hurrying down the stairs*) Serena, have you taken leave of your senses?
SERENA. Not yet, but I'm hoping. In moments of stress, a whisky and soda has been known to have a becalming influence. (*She waves the glass in her left hand*)

(ISABEL *takes the glass from Serena, sniffs the whisky, moves and puts the glass on the table up* L, *then crosses to the light switches up* R *and switches on the wall-brackets*)

ISABEL. So that's it, is it? I don't know what's come over this household. Everyone wandering around in the middle of the night. Now, you go straight up to bed—(*she moves* C) and don't worry about a thing. I'll call you first thing in the morning, and . . . (*For the first time she sees Sir William and stands rooted*)

(SIR WILLIAM *rises*)

Who is this gentleman?

SERENA (*sitting up*) I don't know, but I think he's a poppet, don't you? (*She puts her feet on the coffee table*)

ISABEL. On so short an acquaintance I can't say I've formed an opinion.

(SERENA *giggles*)

(*To Sir William*) Since my daughter appears to be temporarily unhinged, sir, perhaps you would be good enough to inform me who you are, where you come from, and why?

SIR WILLIAM. My name is Barlow, madam.

ISABEL. Barlow. Barlow? I don't know any Barlows.

SIR WILLIAM. Benedick-Barlow, to be precise. I was hyphenated by deed poll at the age of two and a half.

ISABEL. That must have been very unpleasant.

SIR WILLIAM. Far from it. It made me secure and decided my destiny.

ISABEL. How very bizarre. But I'm still in the dark.

SERENA. Aren't we all, aren't we all, aren't we all?

ISABEL (*severely*) Serena, generalizations are tiresome and foolish. Repetition makes them intolerable.

SIR WILLIAM. A philosopher, madam.

ISABEL (*modestly*) One does one's best to adjust to life.

SIR WILLIAM (*with a slight bow*) And succeeds, I've no doubt, and succeeds.

ISABEL (*flattered*) Charming, charming. (*She bows*)

(SIR WILLIAM *bows*)

And now back to work—who are you? We've established that when others were being vaccinated you were being hyphenated. Could we take it from there?

SIR WILLIAM. We are, in fact, strangers. But you may perhaps be familiar with Barlow and Morrison's . . .

ISABEL. Barlow and Morrison's?

SIR WILLIAM. The department store.

ISABEL. Barlow and . . . You're not—(*amazed*) Sir William Barlow?

(SIR WILLIAM *smiles and inclines his head*)

(*Overcome*) My dear Sir William! Oh, but I'm delighted! Really, I am! Do sit down.

(SIR WILLIAM *sits in the easy chair*)

(*She sits on the right arm of the sofa. The gracious hostess*) This *is* a pleasure. Serena, this is Sir William. (*She hastily takes a pair of ear-rings from the pocket of her housecoat and puts them on*) I see it all now, like a great white light. Your firm were late with the wedding gown, so you stopped by in person to make sure they'd come through in the end. But how kind! How extraordinarily kind! The personal touch to end all personal touches. (*She turns to Serena*) Serena, remind me to close my account with Harrods first thing in the morning. (*She rises*) In future, I shall go to Sir William for my every requirement. (*She sits on the sofa at the right end and draws Serena's nightdress down over her legs*) You will forgive us for receiving you in our—(*modestly*) like this, Sir William—but in view of tomorrow's little ceremony we had retired early. (*Aside to Serena*) Sir William's glass is empty, dear.

(SERENA *rises, picks up the whisky bottle from the coffee table and, moving rather carefully, moves round* L *of the sofa, then above it to* C)

(*The perfect hostess making conversation*) And how is *Lady* Barlow?

SIR WILLIAM. I beg your pardon?

ISABEL. Your wife—is she well?

SIR WILLIAM. There is no Lady Barlow, madam. There never has been a Lady Barlow. There never will be a Lady Barlow.

ISABEL. Oh. What a shame.

SIR WILLIAM. On the contrary. What an achievement.

(BARBARA *enters by the upstairs archway, moves to* C *of the balcony and listens, unobserved by the others*)

ISABEL. Really? Then you're a bachelor by conviction?

SIR WILLIAM. One might say from birth. I was not christened "Benedick" for nothing.

ISABEL. *Much Ado About* . . . Ah, yes, I see.

(SERENA *refills Sir William's glass, then crosses above the easy chair, puts the bottle and her glass on the mantelpiece, then sits on the stool down* R)

SIR WILLIAM (*rising*)

"Down to Gehenna or up to the Throne
He travels the fastest who travels—alone."

Kipling.

ISABEL (*rising; not to be outdone*)

"Who travels alone without lover or friend
But hurries from nothing to naught at the end."

Ella Wheeler Wilcox.

(ISABEL *and* SIR WILLIAM *bow to each other*)

BARBARA (*on the balcony*) And *I* know another one.

ISABEL. Barbara!

BARBARA (*not heeding*) "The happy married man dies in good style at home—(*she comes down the stairs*) surrounded by his weeping wife and children, but the old bachelor don't die proper at all. He sort of rots away like a polywog's tail."

ISABEL. Barbara, go to your room.

(SIR WILLIAM *reseats himself in the easy chair*)

BARBARA (*moving down* L *of the sofa*) Artemus Ward said that in eighteen sixty-seven.

ISABEL. I don't care if King Canute said it the day he burnt the cakes.

SERENA. That was Alfred, Mummy.

BARBARA (*crossing above the sofa to* C; *to Sir William*) Good evening. I know your face.

ISABEL. I must apologize for my youngest daughter. (*She gently plucks at Barbara's rear*) Up to bye-byes, darling.

BARBARA. I've seen it before somewhere. Recently. Where have I seen it?

ISABEL (*getting mad*) Barbara Kilpatrick, do you wish me to rouse your father?

BARBARA. I doubt if he'd help.

ISABEL (*sitting on the sofa at the left end*) Sometimes one wonders if the whole idea of procreation wasn't the most ghastly mistake.

BARBARA (*moving down* C) He was in the papers—yesterday—no, the day before.

SERENA (*rising and moving to* R *of Sir William*) Morning or evening?

ISABEL. Serena, support your mother.

BARBARA. Evening. And there was a photograph . . .

ISABEL (*rising*) Barbara, one more word and you go to an approved school. There's an excellent one just outside Tunbridge Wells.

(SERENA *moves to the stool*)

BARBARA (*moving above the easy chair and jumping up and down in excitement*) Wait, it's coming, it's coming, it's coming.

ISABEL (*moving to* L *of the easy chair*) I implore your indulgence, from the bottom of my heart, Sir William.

BARBARA (*pointing at Sir William*) Sir William. Sir William Barlow.

ISABEL. Of course, he's Sir William Barlow. We all know that. (*She moves below the left end of the sofa*)

BARBARA (*with a great cry*) Golly! You're *dead*! (*She points at Sir William and backs to the up* R *corner of the sofa*) He died in the *Evening Standard*—(*she runs down* C) the night before last.

(ISABEL *makes a strange, strangled noise in her throat, moves* C *a step and laughs desperately*)

ISABEL. Youth, Sir William. You know what youth is. No doubt you have girls of your own . . . (*She moves down* L *of the sofa*) My God, he's a bachelor.

BARBARA (*moving to the table behind the sofa*) Where's the *Standard*?

(SERENA *kneels by the stool and puts the magazines and papers from it on to the floor*)

SERENA. Here's tonight's.

(BARBARA *crosses, kneels* L *of Serena and searches through the papers*)

BARBARA. And last night's! Where's the night before's?

ISABEL (*moving to the newel post and leaning against it*) I'm awfully sorry, but I think I'm going to faint.

(*No-one takes any notice of Isabel*)

I say, I think I'm going to faint.

SERENA. Wait, Mummy, not just for a minute.

ISABEL. Wait? I can't wait! I'm going.

BARBARA (*searching among the papers*) Blast! Where is it?

ISABEL (*gravitating upstage to the pillar* LC *and hanging on to it for support*) I've gone!

SERENA (*finding the paper*) Here it is!

ISABEL (*crossing suddenly above the easy chair* RC *and standing above the two kneeling girls*) Where? Where?

BARBARA. It was on the front page.

SERENA (*reading aloud from the newspaper*) "Commercial prince passes on. It is with regret that we announce the death this afternoon of Sir William Benedick-Barlow."

BARBARA. That's him!

SERENA. There's his picture.

(ISABEL *takes her spectacles from her pocket, looks over the girls' shoulders at the picture, then looks aghast at Sir William*)

(*She reads*) "Sir William, who, so far as is known, had been in the best of health, collapsed suddenly while addressing the annual luncheon of the Bachelors' Club, of which he had for so long been the life and soul. The body, which was taken to Charing Cross Hospital . . ."

BARBARA. Turned up later in St John's Wood!

ISABEL (*swaying*) I think I must have a little air. (*She moves to the pillar up* RC, *circles it, then leans against it, groaning*)

SERENA (*reading*) "Sir William was the Chairman of Barlow and Morrison's, and their associated companies, Grant and Hagerley's, Dawson and Atcheson's, Tatham and Brassetts . . ."

ISABEL (*tottering down* C) Help me, ho!

(SIR WILLIAM *rises and turns to Isabel*)

(*She falls on to Sir William's upstage arm*) Oh! How kind. Thank you so much. I . . . (*She suddenly realizes who is supporting her and pulls herself upright*) Oh, my God! (*She faints dead away in Sir William's arms*)

SERENA *and* BARBARA *rise and* BARBARA *runs to* R *of Isabel as—*

the CURTAIN *falls*

ACT II

SCENE—*The same. A few minutes later.*

When the CURTAIN *rises,* ISABEL *is lying back on the sofa, at the right end.* SERENA *is kneeling on the sofa, at the left end.* BARBARA *is standing up* L *of the sofa.*

SERENA. More whisky, Babs. (*She holds out a glass from the coffee table*)

(BARBARA *pours a tot of whisky from the bottle, which during the Interval has been moved from the mantelpiece to the table above the sofa.* SERENA *presses the glass to* ISABEL'S *lips, and she chokes and opens her eyes*)

Better now, Mummy?

(SIR WILLIAM *enters down* R *and crosses to* R *of the sofa. He carries a glass*)

ISABEL (*hoarsely*) I think so, darling. Where is he? Has he gone? Is he . . .?

(SIR WILLIAM *leans over Isabel*)

Oh, my God!
BARBARA (*handing the bottle to Sir William*) Give her another slug.

(ISABEL *gasps and waves the whisky away*)

ISABEL. Don't touch me!

(SIR WILLIAM *chuckles.*
   JASON *enters by the upstairs archway. He wears an Oriental dressing-gown over his pyjamas. He is without his glasses, and is peering at a pocket watch*)

JASON. I say, is it time to get up?
ISABEL. Jason!
JASON (*moving along the balcony*) My watch must have stopped. (*He comes halfway down the stairs*) Now, isn't that a curious thing? The hands pointed distinctly to . . .

(*A clock strikes one*)

Lunchtime already? (*He puts the watch in the breast pocket of his pyjamas*)
SERENA. It's one o'clock in the morning, Daddy.
JASON. What? But, good gracious me, if it's one o'clock in the

morning, then—then who is this gentleman? It is a gentleman, isn't it? I haven't got my glasses. His clothes indicate that he's here for the wedding, but . . . (*He moves above the left end of the sofa*)

ISABEL. Over my dead body. (*To Sir William*) And if you say, "That makes two of us," I'll murder you.

BARBARA (*crossing to L of the easy chair*) Why are you dressed for the wedding?

SIR WILLIAM. These are the clothes I chanced to have on when it happened.

JASON. When what happened?

SIR WILLIAM. Oblivion. That is, of course, in the material sense. (*He crosses to the fireplace and puts the bottle and glass on the mantelpiece*)

JASON (*vaguely*) Ah, yes, of course. (*Aside to Isabel, over the back of the sofa*) What's he talking about? (*He moves to R of the sofa*)

SERENA. You see, Daddy, he was making a speech at a luncheon——

BARBARA. The Bachelors' Club.

SERENA (*crossing and standing down R*) —when he suddenly went out like a light. It's all here in the papers. (*She picks up the newspaper and sits on the right arm of the easy chair*)

BARBARA (*crossing above the easy chair to R of it*) There's a photograph, too. (*She takes the paper from Serena. To Sir William*) You might care to keep it as a souvenir. (*She hands the paper to Sir William, then crosses above the easy chair and sits on the left arm of it*)

SIR WILLIAM. Thank you.

JASON (*floundering*) Isabel, explain.

ISABEL (*taking a deep breath*) Now, Jason, sit down.

(JASON *sits on the sofa,* R *of Isabel*)

I want you to be rather cool and calm and splendid and not get excited. Will you try not to get excited?

(SIR WILLIAM *sits on the stool down* R, *takes a small pair of scissors from his waistcoat pocket and cuts out the excerpt from the paper*)

JASON. I am not in the least excited, my dear. I merely wondered . . .

ISABEL. There's no need to be tetchy, I'm only thinking of your metabolism. Jason—this—is Sir William Barlow.

BARBARA (*looking at Sir William*) The *late* Sir William Barlow.

SERENA (*looking at Sir William*) The late Sir William Benedick-Barlow. There's a hyphen, Daddy.

BARBARA. The hyphen is immaterial.

ISABEL. So is Sir William. You see, Jason?

JASON (*fogged*) No, dear.

ISABEL. I should have thought it was perfectly clear. Sir William Barlow is no longer with us.

Act II   THE BRIDE AND THE BACHELOR

JASON (*baffled*) He seems to be still in the room, dear. That smudge over there.

(*The* GIRLS *look* R)

ISABEL. I believe you're doing it deliberately to annoy me.

(*The* GIRLS *look* L)

(*Loudly and clearly*) Sir William has just passed over. There! Now I've said it.
SERENA (*rising*) The day before yesterday, Daddy.
JASON (*after a moment; puzzled*) Passed over what?
ISABEL. I warn you, Jason, if I once start to scream I shall go on and on and on.

(SERENA *moves to Sir William, takes the cutting from him and moves* C. JASON *rises.* BARBARA *rises and moves between Jason and Serena*)

SERENA (*handing the cutting to Jason*) Here, Daddy.

(JASON *reads the cutting*)

JASON. Ah, tut, tut, tut, m'mm, so that's the ticket. (*He crosses to Sir William and hands him the cutting*)

(SIR WILLIAM *exits down* R)

Well, all I can say is, I should never have known. I mean, it hardly shows at all.

(BARBARA *sits on the right arm of the sofa*)

ISABEL. Jason, we are contemplating a cadaver, not a maternity case.
JASON. I'm aware of the position, my dear.
ISABEL. Then how dare you be so cavalier! (*She rises and moves round* L *of the sofa to* C) Have you no sensibility?
JASON (*moving to* R *of Isabel*) But, my dear, you asked me to keep calm, you asked me particularly.

(SERENA *moves slowly down* R)

ISABEL. I didn't ask you to be calmer than I am. It's extremely bad manners.
JASON. I'm sorry, I . . .
ISABEL. Anyone would think you were in constant communion with the hereafter. Perhaps you . . . (*She breaks off and clutches Jason*)

(SIR WILLIAM *enters down* R. SERENA *watches him*)

JASON (*trying to be social*) Inclement weather.
SIR WILLIAM (*moving* R *of the easy chair*) Chilly.

(Sir William *exits up* R. Serena *moves up* R *and watches Sir William off.* Isabel *sinks into the easy chair and gives way to subdued hysteria*)

Jason. Oh, come, there's no cause for alarm. (*He moves to* L *of Isabel*) He's probably some sort of hallucination.
Serena. He doesn't look like an hallucination to me.

(Isabel *gives an hysterical laugh*)

Jason. Of course, I couldn't see him too clearly without my glasses.
Isabel. Barbara, go and fetch your father's glasses.
Barbara (*rising*) I'll miss something, I'll miss something.
Isabel (*over-riding her*) We'll take careful note of whatever occurs in your absence and give you a full report on your return. (*To Jason*) Where are your glasses?
Jason. On the table beside the bed, dear.
Isabel (*to Barbara, repeating*) On the table beside the bed, dear.
Barbara (*crossing and running up the stairs*) Blast!

(Barbara *exits by the upstairs archway*)

Jason (*moving to* L *of Serena; cautiously*) Where is our friend now?
Serena (*looking off* R) He's gone into the kitchen.
Isabel (*nervously*) What's he doing in there?
Jason (*moving to* L *of Isabel*) Perhaps he feels hungry after his journey. I often get hungry myself going down in a lift.
Isabel. We can't be sure he came down. He may have come up.
Jason. Yes, of course. There is that.
Isabel (*weakly*) Jason, send for a doctor.
Jason. I doubt if even a doctor could bring him round once he's passed over.
Isabel (*exasperated*) For your wife, Jason. Unless you wish me to join him.
Jason (*crossing and standing down* L *of the sofa*) You know, Sir Walter Scott once thought he saw the ghost of Byron at Abbotsford. But it turned out to be a conglomeration of coats that hung in the hall. Raincoats.
Isabel. Are you suggesting that for the past half-hour we've been entertaining a mackintosh?
Jason. The thought crept up my back.
Isabel (*rising and moving* c) Jason, your daughter is to marry in less than twelve hours, and there's a live corpse in the kitchen.
Jason. Yes, I know, dear.
Isabel. Then will you kindly concentrate?
Jason (*crossing down* R; *concentrating hard*) Well, of course, if he's not an hallucination, he may have some reason for coming. If he

Act II THE BRIDE AND THE BACHELOR

does have a reason, we must try to find out what it is. Once we find why he came, we must find him a reason for going.

ISABEL (*impressed*) That's the first piece of logical thinking you've done in twelve months.

(BARBARA *enters by the upstairs arch. She carries Jason's glasses.* SERENA *stands by the pillar up* RC)

JASON. Oh, it shouldn't take that long.
ISABEL. Now you've spoilt it.

(BARBARA *runs down the stairs and crosses to* L *of Isabel*)

BARBARA. They weren't on the table beside the bed. They were in the bathroom on top of Boccaccio. (*She hands the glasses to Isabel*)

ISABEL (*moving below the easy chair*) Thank you, that's quite enough of . . .

(SIR WILLIAM *enters up* R, *carrying a plate of food. He moves down between Isabel and Jason and exits down* R. JASON *and* ISABEL *peer after Sir William.* ISABEL *gives* JASON *his glasses, which he quickly puts on.* SERENA *follows Sir William down* R, *then sits on the stool and looks at the open door*)

JASON. Well, I must say he does seem remarkably solid in texture. I suppose there's no doubt the deceased *is* deceased.
ISABEL. Of course he's deceased. He's as dead as a doornail. (*She moves* C) Though why a doornail . . .
BARBARA (*backing below the coffee table*) That's easy. The doornail was originally the knob on which the knocker struck. As it was constantly being hit on the head it couldn't be said to have much life in it. Other similes——
ISABEL. Thank you. That covers it nicely.
BARBARA (*pressing on, regardless*) —include "Dead as mutton", "Dead as stone", and "Dead as a shotten herring".
JASON (*moving to* R *of Isabel*) I've always felt the analogy with the shotten herring to be a particularly jolly one myself.
ISABEL (*moving below the sofa*) I'm going mad. I'm being driven stark, staring mad in the middle of the night, by my own family, in my own house. (*She sits on the sofa, at the left end*)
JASON (*sitting* R *of Isabel on the sofa*) Chin up, my dear. Try and enter into the *spirit* of the thing.

(ISABEL *gives Jason an old-fashioned look.* BARBARA *sits on the left arm of the sofa*)

ISABEL (*wildly*) How can one enter into the spirit of a spirit?
JASON. Well, I've never tried it myself, but the dim-dims of Northern Natal say it's practically child's play.

(SIR WILLIAM *enters down* R *and stands in the open doorway*)

SIR WILLIAM. I like this house. There's an air of warmth about it. I do like heat. (*He shuts the door*)

ISABEL (*faintly*) I feel hot air rising.

(SIR WILLIAM *moves up* C)

(*She hisses*) Jason, open a window. He wants to go out. Quick!

(SERENA *rises and moves* R *of the easy chair*)

JASON (*rising and moving up* C *to Sir William*) Would you care to see the garden? Of course, it's not at its best in October. You must come again in the Spring.

ISABEL. Jason!

JASON. Ah. Quite so. Would you care for a sherry? (*He moves to the table up* L)

SIR WILLIAM. Thank you.

SERENA (*collecting the bottle and glass from the mantelpiece*) He'd rather have whisky. (*She moves down* C) It burns.

(JASON *moves* C)

SIR WILLIAM (*moving to* L *of Serena and taking the bottle and glass from her*) Alas, no longer, but I'll go through the motions with pleasure.

(SERENA *sits on the floor below the easy chair*. ISABEL *takes a drink from the glass on the coffee table*)

ISABEL. I'll go through them, too.

(SIR WILLIAM *pours a drink for himself, sits on the sofa at the right end, and puts the bottle on the coffee table*)

BARBARA. Up, spirits!

ISABEL. Barbara! (*She puts her glass on the coffee table and accidentally comes in contact with Sir William's elbow*)

SIR WILLIAM. I beg your pardon! (*He drinks*)

ISABEL (*shrinking away from him*) I beg yours. (*She furtively pulls a cushion between them. After a pause*) Are you—are you planning to spend any length of time with us, or is this just a flying visit?

SIR WILLIAM. I wish I knew.

ISABEL. Well, we must just live in hopes, mustn't we?

SIR WILLIAM. Those of us who can. (*He contemplates his drink*)

JASON (*after a pause; suddenly seeing the joke*) Ha! Ha!

(ISABEL *jumps and hiccups*)

Try not to be too downhearted, my dear chap. (*He moves down* C) We all have to go sometime.

ISABEL. But so far as is generally known we don't have to come back.

SERENA (*leaning on her right arm*) Why *have* you come back?

SIR WILLIAM. I was sent. (*He drinks*)

ACT II THE BRIDE AND THE BACHELOR

ISABEL. By whom?

(SIR WILLIAM *looks heavenwards. They all follow his gaze*)

(*With relief*) Ah—then you have come *down*—that is, your sensation was one of *de*scending?

SIR WILLIAM. There *was* no sensation. One moment I was in a remarkably pleasant place. The next, I was here. No offence.

JASON (*sitting in the easy chair; dismissing it*) My dear fellow!

ISABEL. And this visit was not your own personal project?

SIR WILLIAM. My dear lady, the round trip from here to eternity and back is hardly one to be undertaken from choice.

ISABEL. Then why *did* you undertake it?

SIR WILLIAM (*pausing and looking* L *and* R) It was as a result of something I *failed* to do that I was—sent down.

JASON. What did you fail to do, old chap?

(*There is a pause*)

SIR WILLIAM (*at length; flatly*) Get married.
ISABEL (*astonished*) Get married?

(SIR WILLIAM *rises and moves up* C)

JASON. Get married?
SERENA. Get married?
BARBARA. Get married?
SIR WILLIAM. Get married. Shortly after departing this earth the day before yesterday, I found myself seated on a bench immediately outside heaven. With me was the late Headmaster of one of our leading public schools. We were discussing the rise in the cost of dying (*he crosses above the easy chair to* R *of it*) when I was asked to step into the lodge, or dormy house, as they call it. There, in a room with a perfectly heavenly view, I was introduced to a man in a blue lounge suit, who asked me my Christian name. I said it was William, and he said his was Peter, and gave me a cigarette.

(ISABEL *clears her throat, then* JASON, *and finally, louder,* SIR WILLIAM)

Then opening a drawer in a desk—gold, of course——
JASON (*aside*) Of course.
SIR WILLIAM. —he took out a transparent file. This he leafed through quite casually for a moment, then putting it down he said, with an angelic smile, that according to the records I had, and I quote, "a spot of unfinished business to attend to below". I assumed, wrongly, that he was referring to Barlow and Morrison's. I see their shares have dropped to thirty-three and a third by the way. Quite flattering.
JASON (*to Isabel*) Who are Barlow and Morrison's, dear?

ISABEL. You've heard of Swan and Edgar's?
JASON. Ah yes. The biscuit people.

(SIR WILLIAM *coughs at this interruption*)

SIR WILLIAM. Then Peter went on to tell me of the authorities' concern for family life on earth, and in particular a tendency among the more sensitive brides to be struck with confusion and doubt on the eve of the ceremony. (*He looks at Serena*)
ISABEL. Well, of course, every woman has doubts where men are concerned. On the eve of my own wedding I was positively riddled with doubts—most of them entirely justified.
JASON. Oh.
ISABEL. But that's not to say I regret it——
JASON. Thank you, dear.
ISABEL. —altogether.
SIR WILLIAM. Where was I?
SERENA. Struck with confusion and doubt on the eve of the ceremony.
SIR WILLIAM (*crossing above the easy chair to* C) Thank you. Well, it seems it's become recent practice, whenever a bachelor reaches the heavenly gates, to send the poor devil straight back to earth, and not to let him in again until he's steadied the last-minute nerves of some bride-to-be and seen that she marries her man in the manner appointed. By ensuring another's union to make up for not having united himself, so to speak. For so long as she needs him, he must act as her "guardian angel". Nor may he show his face again at the gates of heaven until his work has been wholly —and holily—done. (*He sits on the sofa at the right end*)
JASON. Well, I'm blessed!

(SERENA *rises, crosses to the mantelpiece, and stands with her back to the room*)

ISABEL (*suddenly*) So *that's* how they put the guts back into Monica Bulstrode.
SIR WILLIAM. Monica . . .?
ISABEL. Bulstrode. A large girl with strong teeth.
BARBARA. And a big bust.
ISABEL. I don't know if you've met her?
SIR WILLIAM. I think not.
ISABEL. You'd know if you had. A week before her wedding she came out in the most peculiar rash, from head to toe. At first they thought it was German measles—her young man came from Munich—but it turned out to be a violent attack of pre-nuptial nerves.
SIR WILLIAM. There are countless examples all over the world, so they tell me.

ACT II THE BRIDE AND THE BACHELOR 37

ISABEL. The poor girl was so petrified it was clear that if she got to the church at all it would only be on a stretcher.

(SERENA *sits in the armchair up* R)

But lo and behold she bounced down the aisle like a football, and now there are six enormous children, and two more on the way—so the doctor says. I'm convinced she was taken in hand by some heavenly body.
SIR WILLIAM. There's no question about it.
JASON (*rising*) Amazing, amazing! And you say *all* bachelors are required to make this—excursion?
SIR WILLIAM. All those who have remained single by conviction and not force of circumstance.
ISABEL. We'd better warn old Uncle Aubrey. He's ninety on Thursday. Never mind, he'll just have to pull up his socks and start courting.
BARBARA (*logically*) What about spinsters?
SIR WILLIAM. I didn't enquire, but I've no doubt the same rule applies.
JASON. Oh, but I say, this is capital, capital! (*He moves above the easy chair*)
ISABEL. Jason, contain yourself.
JASON. No, but really, my dear, it's so very heart-warming to find that the old tradition of "bouncing the bachelor" still endures. (*He moves down* R *of the easy chair*) It gives one a sense of continuity.
ISABEL. It's given me a headache. (*She rises, moves round* L *of the sofa, picks up the bowl and the book, "Doors of Perception"*)
SIR WILLIAM (*rising and turning to Serena; briskly*) Well, now, to work. Young woman, come here.

(SERENA *rises*)

ISABEL (*moving* C) Serena, remain where you are.

(SERENA *resumes her seat*)

Sir William, I'm sure we're all very grateful to you for taking the trouble to come all this long way, but there is no problem in this house, apart from my husband. So will you kindly go back and report that there's been a mistake.
SIR WILLIAM. There is no mistake, I assure you. A call for help came from this address on the stroke of midnight, your time.
ISABEL (*putting the book on the table behind the sofa; to Jason*) You've finally gone too far.
JASON. My dear, I made no call.
SIR WILLIAM (*picking up the bottle and glass and moving to* L *of the sofa*) Well, somebody did. "Quel atranta, quel atronta, quel atronta, quel atrine."

(ISABEL *moves to the fireplace, then goes down* R, *holding up the bowl, where Sir William's quotation causes her to halt abruptly*)

Someone in this house spoke those words at exactly twelve o'clock midnight.

ISABEL (*dropping the bowl; faintly*) Jason.

JASON. Another window, my dear?

(SIR WILLIAM *puts the bottle and glass on the table up* L)

SERENA. Mummy, what is it?

ISABEL. It's me. It's me. (*She wails*) I'm a dim-dim! (*She collapses into the easy chair*)

(SERENA *rises, picks up the bowl and puts it on the stool*)

BARBARA (*rising and crossing to* R *of the sofa*) Well, blow me down! (*She sits on the right arm of the sofa*)

ISABEL (*hysterically*) I'm a dim-dim! I'm a dim-dim!

(SERENA *sits on the floor* R *of the easy chair*)

JASON (*sitting on the left arm of the easy chair*) Oh, come now. Cheer up, chicken. You've got magic fingers. I'm not sure you oughtn't to be rather proud.

ISABEL (*wildly*) Proud? Proud? To find out I'm a *witch*!

JASON (*cheerfully*) Not to worry, not to worry.

SERENA. Darling, don't be upset. You're a modern Merlin.

BARBARA (*rising and crossing above the easy chair to* R *of it*) And if it's hereditary, I'm one, too. (*She sits on the right arm of the easy chair*) We can work together.

ISABEL (*with her arms around Barbara and Serena; choked*) You're all being terribly sweet and—and kind—and—and loyal—but I know how you really feel. (*She buries her head on Jason's chest*) I—I'm so *ashamed*.

SIR WILLIAM (*exploding*) All this is entirely beside the point. (*He moves down* L *of the sofa. To Serena*) Young woman, you have, I gather, a problem.

(SERENA *rises*)

I am here, if I can, to resolve it.

ISABEL. Sir William . . .

SIR WILLIAM (*thundering*) Silence, madam. (*To Serena. Quietly*) What is it?

SERENA. N-nothing.

BARBARA. Go on, you might as well tell.

(*There is a pause.* SERENA *crosses to* R *of Sir William*)

SERENA (*in a small voice*) Well—I keep dreaming treble.

JASON (*rising*) Keep doing what, dear?

SERENA (*sitting on the sofa at the right end*) My—my thoughts—my innermost feelings—keep coming in threes.

(SIR WILLIAM *sits on the sofa,* L *of Serena and takes a pocketbook and pencil from his pocket*)

SIR WILLIAM. Tell me. Tell me your dream.
SERENA (*after a pause; slowly*) Well, first of all it was jam-jars.
SIR WILLIAM (*making notes*) Jam-jars.

(JASON *sits on the left arm of the easy chair*)

SERENA. Three jam-jars in a row. Then—three pencils.
SIR WILLIAM. Pencils . . .?
SERENA. Three pencils that walked.
SIR WILLIAM (*impressed*) Really?
SERENA. Then three ships with three funnels.
SIR WILLIAM. What line?
SERENA. I don't remember. Always three. Three of everything.
ISABEL. With a father in the Civil Service, what else do you expect? (*She rises, crosses and sits on the right arm of the sofa*) You never told mummy. Why didn't you come to mummy?
SERENA. I didn't mind it at first. I even thought it was sort of amusing. But then came the wedding. That's when it began to get serious.
JASON. Wedding? What wedding?
ISABEL. Hers, of course. Sssh!
SERENA. I came down the aisle and—and there were three at the altar, where you only expect to find one.
JASON. Three clergy?
SERENA. No. Three bridegrooms.
BARBARA. In three tail coats.
SERENA. With three rings.
BARBARA. And three red carnations.
JASON. How does she know they were red?
ISABEL. She was dreaming in Technicolor. Be quiet!
SERENA. They made the responses in unison, right through the service. And when it came to the taking of vows, they all said— (*she intones*) "We do", "We do", "We do"—like the Beverley Sisters. I had that one three nights running. (*Shyly*) Then came the prams.
ISABEL. Prams?

(*They all look at Serena*)

BARBARA. She was out with the kids in the Park.
JASON. Which Park?
SERENA. Hyde Park.
JASON. Hyde Park?
SERENA. It must have been Hyde Park because I could see Battersea Power Station in the distance.
BARBARA (*rising and sitting in the easy chair*) You can't see Battersea Power Station from Hyde Park.

ISABEL. It must have been Green Park.
JASON. You can, Babs dear.
ISABEL (*rising*) Oh, no, you can't.
JASON (*rising*) Oh, yes.

(ISABEL *resumes her seat*)

I remember standing just to the right of the Marble Arch on a wet Sunday in nineteen fifty-two, and thinking, "Hallo, hallo, why there's the Battersea Power Station." (*He sits on the left arm of the easy chair*)

ISABEL ⎫ ⎧Nonsense!
BARBARA ⎬(*together*) ⎨Impossible!
SERENA ⎭ ⎩That's right.

JASON (*sticking to his guns*) I remember distinctly. It depressed me. And there were all those jolly little ducks on the Round Pond to the left of us. Quack-quack! Quack-quack!

ISABEL (*impatiently*) Quack-quack! Quack-quack! That was Hampstead Heath.

JASON (*rising, crossing above the easy chair and standing down* R) No, my dear. Hyde Park.

(ISABEL *rises and moves below the easy chair*)

(*He looks at Isabel*) Or—wait a minute now—was it St James's?

SIR WILLIAM (*rising, in exasperation*) Would it be asking too much if we stuck to the point for five consecutive seconds?

ISABEL (*with dignity*) Really, Sir William, there's no need to shout. You may be a voice from the grave, but you're coming through perfectly.

JASON. No, I'm sure it was Hyde Park because of the tulips.

(BARBARA *rises and moves between Jason and Isabel*)

ISABEL. What month?
JASON. April.
ISABEL. Daffodils.
JASON. No, no, I'm convinced that . . .
ISABEL. Jason, we don't give a hoot if it was the Hog's Back, Newlands Corner, or Whipsnade Zoo.
JASON. It can't have been Whipsnade. I haven't been down there for years.
SERENA. Anyway, there I was with three prams—and three babies.
ISABEL. Whose babies?
SERENA. Mine, of course.
ISABEL (*sitting in the easy chair; sentimentally*) Ah, the darlings!
BARBARA. Boys or girls?
SERENA. I don't know. They just seemed to be—babies.
JASON. I hope they were boys. I've always wanted boys in the family.

ACT II THE BRIDE AND THE BACHELOR 41

SIR WILLIAM (*with feeling*) You have my profound understanding.
BARBARA. We resent that!
(ISABEL, SERENA *and* BARBARA *glower at Sir William*)
SERENA. Where was I?
ISABEL. Pushing three babies in three perambulators across some stretch of greensward which shall be nameless.
(BARBARA *sits on the right arm of the easy chair*)
SERENA. That's right. They were laughing and gurgling and waving their arms at their daddies.
ISABEL. How many daddies?
SERENA. Three, of course.
ISABEL. And only one mummy? That seems excessive.
BARBARA. One pop per pram.
JASON (*crossing above the easy chair to* R *of the sofa*) Who were they, my dear? Did you recognize them?
SERENA. Of course. I was married to them, wasn't I?
ISABEL. Well, I sincerely ... You know, you've got me so morally confused I don't even know what to *hope*.
JASON (*to Barbara*) Who are the three daddies she's supposed to be married to?
BARBARA (*sitting on the floor down* R) Joe, Simon and Scotty.
ISABEL (*shaken to the core*) Oh, *no*, Serena!
JASON. Now where have I heard those names before?
SERENA. So you do see it's desperate, don't you?
SIR WILLIAM. Who are Joe, Simon and Scotty?
BARBARA. Joe's the bridegroom.
ISABEL. Poor dear Joe.
BARBARA. Simon's best man, and Scotty's chief usher.
JASON (*moving up* R *of the table above the sofa*) I knew I'd heard those names somewhere. Good fellows.
ISABEL. They're all devoted.
SIR WILLIAM. To whom?
ISABEL. To each other.
BARBARA. And to Serena.
SERENA (*miserably*) I can't marry Joe and be faithless to him in my sleep. And I can't stay awake for ever. What *am* I to do?
BARBARA (*helpfully*) Can't she marry all three?
ISABEL (*rising*) No, she cannot marry all three.
SERENA. But, Mummy ...
ISABEL (*crossing to* L *of the sofa; firmly*) I'm sorry, my darling. I understand your position, and I'm not saying there isn't a lot to be said for it—there are times when I'd welcome a wider selection myself—(*she looks darkly at Jason*) but you'll just have to settle for one at a time like the rest of us.

JASON (*moving above the easy chair; mildly*) I once dreamt I had six wives. I've often wondered what it meant.

(JASON *catches* ISABEL'S *eye. She withers him with a glance. He tries to look nonchalant, and attempts to put his hands into the non-existent pockets of his dressing-gown*)

ISABEL (*darkly*) I shall be happy to discuss its meaning at your earliest convenience.

BARBARA (*rising and sitting on the right arm of the easy chair*) Sometimes dreams go by opposites. Maybe she's allergic.

(JASON *moves to* R *of the easy chair*)

ISABEL. Allergic to what?
BARBARA. Marriage.
SERENA. I'm *not* allergic. I love Joe, I feel an affinity for him.
ISABEL. Then for heaven's sake trust your affinity and let's get some sleep.
SERENA. But it isn't exclusive. I'm full of affinities.
ISABEL. How many?
SERENA (*miserably*) Three.
ISABEL (*throwing up her hands and moving up* C) I give up.
SIR WILLIAM (*rising and moving to the table up* L) My sentiments exactly.
ISABEL (*turning*) What?
SIR WILLIAM. I should like to take this opportunity of saying that, being in my right mind and fully aware of the consequences of my action—I, too, give up. (*He pours a stiff drink for himself*)

(SERENA *lies on the sofa with her head at the left end.* BARBARA *rises, then sits in the easy chair, with her head on her left arm*)

ISABEL (*alarmed*) But you can't. Your mission. You'll be permanently displaced.

SIR WILLIAM. If one's hopes of heaven depend upon injecting some measure of sanity into a madhouse—(*he turns to Isabel*) one has no alternative but to go to the devil. Your very good health! (*He drinks*)

ISABEL (*breaking to* R *and returning to* C) Well! That's a pretty speech! You come roaring back from heaven knows where, merely to wangle yourself a pass into Paradise, and, at the first sign of rough weather, you give up the ghost.

SIR WILLIAM. May I point out that I did not ask to come back, I was chosen?

ISABEL. A more unfortunate choice one can scarcely imagine.

SIR WILLIAM (*controlling himself with difficulty*) May I also be permitted to state my considered opinion that Freud, Jung and Adler, acting in close concert with every saint in the calendar,

ACT II THE BRIDE AND THE BACHELOR 43

would make about as much impression on this household as a tsetse fly on the skin of a school of rhinoceros.

(SERENA *sits up*)

JASON (*picking up the bowl from the stool*) I see his point, you know, Isabel. (*He puts the bowl on the floor and sits on the stool*) We're not easy.

SIR WILLIAM. If you had anything remotely practical to suggest . . .

ISABEL (*hotly*) I suggest you lay off the booze, before you drink yourself into an early grave, that's what I suggest.

SIR WILLIAM (*with dignity*) I go through the motions, nothing more. It's a reflex action.

ISABEL. You can tell that to Oliver Cromwell.

SIR WILLIAM. I shall be glad to, if and when I run into him.

ISABEL. Oh, don't be so pompous! (*She moves* R *and turns. Pleading*) There must be something you can do for us.

SIR WILLIAM (*moving up* L *of the easy chair*) I doubt it. Your daughter is, without question, mentally unbalanced. For this she is in no way to blame. With progressive insanity almost a family tradition——

(BARBARA *sits up*)

—the poor child had no chance. No chance whatever.

SERENA (*rising and moving to* L *of Sir William; furiously*) How *dare* you say that! How dare you, how dare you, how dare you! Mummy and daddy have been absolutely *angelic* from the moment I was born. Well, from the day daddy bumped into the bundle that was me on the doorstep of Number Sixty-nine Portland Place.

(ISABEL *moves to* L *of Jason and puts her arm around his shoulder*)

I've had everything that a girl could possibly wish for, just as if I were really their daughter.

(SIR WILLIAM *turns slowly to Serena*)

They've been perfect angels. (*To Jason and Isabel*) Angels, angels —that's how I think of you both—as angels. (*To Sir William*) And as for you—all I can say to you is—why don't you just drop dead? (*She bursts into tears, moves and sits on the sofa at the left end*)

ISABEL (*crossing to Serena*) Serena—darling . . .

BARBARA (*overlapping*) Everyone gets so excited.

ISABEL (*sitting* R *of Serena on the sofa and consoling her*) There, there, my darling. Mummy's here. (*Over her right shoulder*) Really, Sir William, why *don't* you? (*She turns to Serena*) It's all right, my precious, mummy's here.

SIR WILLIAM (*moving* R *of the sofa; in an odd voice*) Did you say —Portland Place?

ISABEL (*picking up the glass of whisky from the coffee table; to Serena*) Here, darling, go through the motions for mummy.

SIR WILLIAM (*faintly*) Number—*Sixty-nine*—Portland Place?

ISABEL (*impatiently*) Yes—yes. It's the Turkish Embassy. My husband dropped by one morning to arrange a lecture on Morris Dancing.

(SIR WILLIAM *crosses above the sofa towards the table up* L, *puts his glass on the table above the sofa in passing, then continues to the newel post.* SERENA *drinks*)

And there was Serena on the Embassy steps, the tiniest little bundle you ever saw in your life, with a thousand pounds in notes pinned to her shawl. (*To Serena*) Better now? (*She takes the glass and puts it on the coffee table*) That's a good girl. (*To Sir William*) The press were delighted. They called her "the thousand pound baby". It was quite a little celebrity we adopted, quite a little celeb—— (*She looks at Sir William*) Sir William, are you feeling quite fit? He's as white as a sheet.

BARBARA. He was white when he got here.

ISABEL. He's gone even whiter.

JASON (*rising and moving to* R *of the easy chair*) My dear chap, I do hope it's nothing serious.

(SIR WILLIAM *appears visibly shaken, and stares down at* SERENA, *whose sobs have suddenly stilled. She stares back at Sir William, wide-eyed*)

SIR WILLIAM (*hoarsely*) The—the thousand pound baby?

ISABEL. Yes. A crude label, but apt.

(SERENA *rises with her hands outstretched and takes a step towards Sir William*)

Are you all right, Serena? (*She pauses*) Serena!

SERENA (*moving back a step, as if hypnotized*) I'm going backwards, Mummy.

ISABEL (*rising*) Are you, dear? Where?

SERENA (*in a strange voice*) I don't know—backwards—backwards—— (*She leans backwards*)

(ISABEL *supports Serena with her hands*)

—backwards—tremendously fast . . .

(BARBARA *rises, then sits on the back of the easy chair with her feet on the seat, to get a better view*)

ISABEL. Jason, stop her! She's talking like Mary Rose.

JASON (*at a loss*) How—what . . .?

ISABEL. *Do* something. *Function!*

JASON (*moving to* R *of Isabel and putting his arm on her back*) I—I don't know what's called for.

ACT II THE BRIDE AND THE BACHELOR 45

SERENA (*stepping to Sir William; tremulously*) I do. I'll say it.
SIR WILLIAM (*frightened*) No! No!
SERENA. I must—Father.
ISABEL. *Father?*

(SERENA *moves slightly to* R *of Sir William, then turns and faces Isabel and Jason*)

SERENA. Don't be frightened . . . Mummy—Daddy—this is Father.

(SIR WILLIAM *sways backwards and forwards*)

BARBARA (*rising and standing on the seat of the easy chair; excitedly*) Look out, he's going. He's going . . .

(SIR WILLIAM *sways below the left end of the sofa and faints backwards on to it, his outstretched right arm taking* ISABEL *down with him. As they collapse,* SERENA *moves down* L *of the sofa, and* JASON *moves up* R *of it*)

He's gone! (*She jumps from the chair*)

(SERENA *moves and kneels on the floor beside Sir William*)

JASON (*looking at Sir William*) You know, I *thought* I detected a likeness.
BARBARA. He's a deadringer.
JASON. The eyes . . .
BARBARA. The nose . . .
ISABEL (*gasping*) The body . . . (*She struggles to extricate herself from under Sir William's arm*)
JASON. No, I think the eyes have it.

(ISABEL *slithers on to her knees and crawls to* R *of the sofa, where* JASON *helps her to rise*)

ISABEL (L *of Jason*) What have I done to deserve this?

(BARBARA *crosses above the sofa to* L *of it*)

JASON (*with his arm around Isabel; philosophizing*) All a part of life's pageant, my dear. "Man was born to trouble as the sparks fly upwards." Ah—downwards, in this case, of course.
SERENA (*looking at Sir William*) Poor darling.

(ISABEL *totters up* R *of the sofa, with* JASON *following*)

BARBARA (*rubbing Sir William's left hand*) He's as cold as the devil. Well, natch. He's gone over.
ISABEL. One more crack and you join him! (*She looks at Serena*) How—how did she know?
SERENA (*desperately massaging Sir William's right hand*) I don't know, I just suddenly did.

JASON. Telepathic communication between the closely related ...
BARBARA (*suddenly*) He's coming round.
ISABEL. What?
SERENA (*rising*) Quick, Babs! The whisky.

(BARBARA *moves to the table up* L *and picks up the bottle of whisky and a glass.* SERENA *crosses to* L *of the sofa*)

ISABEL. Not another drop! (*She snatches the bottle and glass from Barbara*)

(SIR WILLIAM *stirs*)

BARBARA (*moving above the left end of the sofa*) Here he comes again.
JASON. Staggering! Staggering!
SIR WILLIAM (*opening his eyes; hoarsely*) W-where is she?
SERENA (*leaning over the left arm of the sofa*) Here, Father. How do you feel?
SIR WILLIAM (*closing his eyes*) Faint.
ISABEL. I'm fainter. (*She pours the remainder of the whisky into the glass and drinks*)
SERENA (*distracted*) Oh, we *must* bring him round. There's something I've *got* to know.

(ISABEL *puts the bottle on the table above the sofa*)

BARBARA. What?
SERENA (*simply*) If he's father—who's mother?

(ISABEL *and* JASON *look at each other and then at Sir William. They all bend closer to him*)

SIR WILLIAM (*suddenly opening his eyes*) Her name was—Nellie. We met—just once. At a gathering of the Underclothing Association—in Manchester.

(SERENA *kneels on the floor* L *of Sir William*)

It—rained—for two solid weeks. We were—forced to remain—under cover.
JASON (*sympathetically*) Ah! The weather. Responsible for so much that's irregular in these Islands. I recall a certain downfall in Dunoon—her name was Dolly ... (*He catches Isabel's eye, starts, then subsides like a pricked balloon*)
ISABEL (*scathingly*) Shall we not discuss the rake's progress in front of the children?
SIR WILLIAM (*his voice growing fainter*) She wrote—of your impending ... I sent—money. She returned it—and the baby—to Number Sixty-nine—my house—Number Seventy—there was fog—fog ... (*His voice trails away and his eyes close*)
BARBARA. He's gone again.

ACT II THE BRIDE AND THE BACHELOR 47

SERENA. Oh, can't we do something? (*She takes Sir William's hands*) He's freezing.
ISABEL (*putting the glass on the table above the sofa; briskly*) Jason, hot-water bottles.
JASON. Pronto! Pronto!

(JASON *bustles off up* R)

ISABEL. Barbara, hot milk.
BARBARA (*crossing above the sofa to* C) He'd do better on hooch.
ISABEL (*giving Barbara a push*) Don't argue. Into the kitchen.

(BARBARA *exits up* R)

SERENA. He's deathly pale, Mummy.
ISABEL (*leaning over the right arm of the sofa; soothingly*) Now, now, darling—he's a much better colour. See, that alabaster shade has given way to quite a respectable puce. I think we can safely say the worst is over.

(JOE TILNEY *appears at the french windows. He is a simple, clean-cut American in his early thirties. He wears sports flannels and a thick coloured sweater and carries his jacket and a bottle of whisky. It is clear that the stag party has been a success, but* JOE *is well under control*)

JOE (*waving the bottle*) Hi, Momsy-womsy. (*He comes into the room and stands up* C)
ISABEL (*rooted*) Joe!
JOE (*to Serena*) Hi, sugar-plum!
SERENA (*rising and moving above the sofa to* L *of Joe*) Joe! Go away!

(ISABEL *moves down* R)

JOE (*amiably*) Well, now, is that any way for a spousie-wousie to talk to her old man?
ISABEL (*moving swiftly to* R *of Joe*) Joe, Serena is not yet your spousie-wousie.
JOE (*wanting to love everybody*) What's an hour here and there to the kid with the arrows?
ISABEL. Furthermore, if you don't get the hellsie-wellsie out of this housie-wousie, I give you my solemn word she shall enter a nunnery.
JOE (*bewildered*) Look, I'm on my way home—I see lights on —I figure . . .
ISABEL (*with superb hauteur*) Joseph, you've been drinking.
JOE. Like I told you, we passed it around a little . . .
ISABEL (*firmly*) Good *night*, Joseph.
JOE. But, Momsy . . .
ISABEL. I *said*, "Good night."
JOE (*hurt*) If that's the way you want it . . .

ISABEL (*moving down* R) It most certainly is.

(BARBARA *runs in up* R)

BARBARA (*as she enters*) Pop's boiling the pasteurized. (*She sees Joe*) Holy catfish!

JOE (*crossing to* R *of the sofa and looking at Sir William; sympathetically*) Some lush bin takin' a load on? (*He waves the bottle*)

BARBARA (*moving to* R *of Joe and grabbing the bottle*) No, but thanks for the tipsy. (*She sits on the sofa* R *of Sir William, and pours some whisky into the glass on the coffee table*)

JOE. Hey!

SERENA (*moving to* L *of the sofa*) I'll do it.

BARBARA (*pouring more whisky into the glass*) Better make it a stiff one. (*She hands the glass to Serena and puts the bottle on the coffee table*)

ISABEL (*reacting*) Stiff one—Barbara!

BARBARA. Unintentional!

SERENA (*leaning over Sir William*) Here, Father.

ISABEL. Father!

JOE (*moving to* L *of Isabel*) What kind of a deal . . .? Did she say "Father"?

ISABEL (*leading Joe to the french windows*) Never mind what *she* said, *I* said, "Good night." (*She moves to the fireplace*)

JOE (*following Isabel*) Just a minute. Hold everything. Don't tell me *this* is the bum who dumps little babies on doorsteps.

ISABEL (*moving down* R) Now, Joe dear . . .

JOE (*moving* C; *building a slow burn*) I've been wanting to meet this guy for a long time.

ISABEL. Joseph, will you please go home.

JOE (*putting his jacket on the easy chair*) I'm on my way, Momsy, I'm on my way—(*he roars*) just as soon as I've socked Casanova here right on the snoot.

(SERENA *runs above the sofa to* L *of Joe*)

BARBARA (*excitedly*) He's gonna poke his pa-in-law in the puss.

ISABEL. He is *not* going to poke his pa-in-law . . . He's not his pa-in-*law*.

SERENA. Joe, go away. Go away.

JOE (*roaring*) I'm going to kick Daddy-Long-Legs from here to kingdom come.

ISABEL. That will not be necessary, he knows the route backwards.

SERENA. Joe, you lay a finger on father, I'll kill you.

ISABEL (*calling for help*) Jason!

SERENA. I'll tear you limb from limb.

ISABEL (*calling*) Jason.

(JASON *enters hurriedly up* R. *He carries two hot-water bottles*)

ACT II THE BRIDE AND THE BACHELOR 49

JASON (*to Serena*) Here we are. The Kumfi-Kosi and the Kuddlemi-Klutchmi.

(SERENA *takes the bottles, moves down* L *of the sofa and puts the bottles beside Sir William*)

SERENA (*to Joe*) I'll kill you! Kill you! Kill you!
JASON (R *of Joe*) Kill who?
JOE. Now you look here . . .
JASON (*slapping Joe on the back*) Ah, Joseph. Back with the milk in a jiffy.

(JASON *bustles off up* R)

SERENA. Kill you till you're dead, do you hear me?
JOE (*furiously*) Okay, okay—okay. (*He picks up his whisky bottle, goes to the table up* L, *picks up a glass and pours himself a drink*)

(ISABEL *sits in the armchair up* R. SERENA *kneels on the floor* L *of Sir William.* JOE *moves* C *and drinks. Silence descends for a moment*)

ISABEL (*with relief; quietly*) Okay.
JOE (*after a pause; bitterly*) So how come he showed?
ISABEL. I beg your pardon?
JOE. Goldilocks—where'd he come from?
BARBARA (*pointing upwards*) Well, as a matter of fact . . .
ISABEL (*rising and moving above the easy chair*) Barbara! (*She thinks rapidly*) As a matter of fact, Goldilocks—Sir William—has turned up unexpectedly—from Australia.
JOE. In the middle of the night?
ISABEL. It's noon in Sydney. He hasn't had time to adjust to Greenwich Mean Time. (*On the beam now*) The shock of seeing Serena has temporarily prostrated him.
BARBARA. *That's* understandable.
SERENA. Shut up, Babs.
ISABEL. Anyway, he's just returned from down-under.

(JASON *enters up* R. *He carries a small tray on which there is a steaming beaker of milk*)

JASON. Cooking sherry and milk. Piping hot.
ISABEL (*taking the glass*) Just what I wanted. (*She sips the milk*)
JASON (*moving down* R) My dear, that was for Swan and Edgar. (*He shrugs and puts the tray on the stool*)
JOE (*smouldering*) Leaving babies on doorsteps.
ISABEL. Now, Josie-wosie . . .
JOE. That's a hell of a thing, leaving babies on doorsteps. (*He refills his glass*)
SERENA (*impatiently*) It wasn't father who left me on the doorstep. It was mother.
JOE (*moving to* R *of the sofa; belligerently*) Who says so?
BARBARA. He does.
JOE (*belligerently; at Sir William*) Passin' the buck, huh?

ISABEL. No. Passing the baby. (*She smiles at her own adroitness*)
JOE. I don't get it. (*He puts the glass on the table above the sofa*)
ISABEL. Oh, don't you? Let me explain. Do sit down. (*She moves to Joe, pushes him down on to the right arm of the sofa, then sits on the left arm of the easy chair*) Well, now, it seems that Sir William lived at Number Seventy Portland Place, and by an unfortunate error Serena was placed on the steps of Number Sixty-nine. It was his baby, but Mrs—Miss—the young woman, made a mistake in the fog. (*She coughs and sips the milk*)

(JOE *looks bewildered*)

You may recall that a certain Miss Prism, in *The Importance of Being Ernest*, made a similar gaffe, with the result that John Gielgud was found in a handbag at Waterloo.
SERENA. Victoria.
BARBARA. Charing Cross.
ISABEL (*appealing*) Jason.
JASON. I had an idea it was St Pancras.
ISABEL (*rising and picking up Joe's jacket*) Anyway, the poor woman got muddled. It's the sort of thing that could happen to any of us. (*She throws the jacket at Joe*) And now, will you please go home. (*She crosses to the fireplace and puts the beaker on the mantelpiece*)
JOE (*rising and moving reluctantly up* C) Back home we'd send for the sheriff . . . (*A fresh thought strikes him and he turns to Isabel*) Hey! What became of her mom?

(ISABEL *glares at Joe*)

For gosh sakes, moms are important. Leastways, they are in the States.
ISABEL (*sitting in the easy chair; at the end of her tether*) Moms are absolutely essential all over, but this particular mom appears to have disappeared without trace.
JOE. You mean she just dumped the kid and took off?
JASON. So it seems.
JOE (*throwing his jacket on to the easy chair; roaring*) That's a helluva thing! Dumping babies in Portland Place. Goddam it, it's un-American. (*He picks up his glass*)
ISABEL. It's not essentially British, either. At least, not so close to Broadcasting House.
JOE. She could at least have pushed the bell and said, "Hey, here's Junior."
ISABEL. I expect she felt shy.
JOE (*returning to the attack*) And *he* never came forward.
ISABEL. The publicity, you know . . .
JOE. What a heel! I oughta poke him right in . . .
BARBARA (*suddenly*) He's coming round. He's coming round.

(ISABEL *rises quickly, moves to* BARBARA, *pulls her to her feet, passes her across to* RC, *then sits* R *of Sir William on the sofa*)

ISABEL. Now, careful. Don't crowd him. Give him air.
SERENA (*tenderly*) Hallo, dearest Father.
(JOE *sits on the left arm of the easy chair*)
ISABEL. There, there, Sir William.
(SIR WILLIAM *opens his eyes*)
Feeling better?
(SIR WILLIAM *looks blankly at Isabel, then looks around*)
SIR WILLIAM. Where am I?
ISABEL. Where are you? (*She looks at Jason*) Acacia Road, St John's Wood.
JASON. N.W.
ISABEL. Eight.
SIR WILLIAM (*looking at Isabel*) Who are you, madam?
ISABEL. Who am I? Isabel Kilpatrick. (*Deliberately*) Isabel Matilda Kilpatrick. Known as "Waltzing Matilda" to the boys of the Great Outback.
JASON. Out back?
SIR WILLIAM (*bewildered*) Out back where?
ISABEL (*intently*) Out back in your native *Australia*.
SIR WILLIAM. Australia? I know nothing of Australia.
ISABEL (*to Joe*) He's delirious.
SERENA (*rising*) Father, you remember *me*?
ISABEL. Yes, you remember your daughter, Sir William?
SIR WILLIAM. Which daughter, madam?
ISABEL. Your *only* daughter. Or did you also run into wet weather in Sheffield and Leeds?
SIR WILLIAM. I have no daughter.
SERENA (*backing away* L) Father!
SIR WILLIAM. I am, as always, a bachelor. (*He rises and moves* L *of the sofa*)
BARBARA (*moving up* R *of the easy chair*) Oh, brother!
JOE (*rising; with a roar*) I'm gonna do it. I'm gonna pop him right where it hurts.
JASON (*crossing to* R *of Joe, restraining him*) Hold hard! Hold hard!

(SIR WILLIAM *moves up* L *of the table above the sofa and takes a sheaf of notes from his pocket*)

SIR WILLIAM. Gentlemen: before closing my address to you, at this the annual luncheon of our Bachelors' Club——
(JOE *moves towards Sir William*)
JASON. Luncheon? Club?
ISABEL (*rising*) He's gone back four days. (*She crosses to* R *of Jason*)
SIR WILLIAM (*ignoring the interruptions*)—it is my presidential

duty, nay, my delight, to remind you of the torment, the horror, the unparallelled disaster, of what is laughingly called "connubial bliss".

SERENA (*moving on to the bottom step of the stairs*) We'd better get him upstairs.

ISABEL (*sitting on the left arm of the easy chair*) Upstairs? Are you raving?

(JASON *moves above the easy chair.* JOE *moves up* C)

SIR WILLIAM. Bachelors! Brothers! What is our battle cry? (*He moves* R *of the table above the sofa*) "Down with Marriage."

JASON. Ho, ho!

SIR WILLIAM. Sever the Nuptial Knot.

JASON. Ha!

SIR WILLIAM. Burn the Bridal Bed.

JASON. I say, Steady the Buffs.

SIR WILLIAM (*putting his notes on the table above the sofa*) How, you ask, can man triumph over nature? Divert, canalize, sublimate, gentlemen. It can, it *has* been done. I, William Benedick-Barlow, am the living proof.

(*There is a sudden flash of lightning, followed at once by a loud clap of thunder. The wind starts to howl and continues until the end of the Act*)

JASON (*crossing down* R) Thunder, by thunder!

(*There is another flash of lightning and a crash of thunder.* SERENA *screams and runs to* JASON. BARBARA *jumps on to the easy chair.* JOE *breaks below the pillar up* RC)

ISABEL (*rising and crossing to Sir William*) Thunder? It's rage in heaven. (*To Sir William. Deliberately*) Your mission! Your mission! For God's sake, remember your mission.

SIR WILLIAM (*resuming his address*) This *is* my mission. To wed—or not to wed. That is the question.

ISABEL. No, no! You've got the wrong text. (*She points to him*) Where would Adam have been without Eve?

SIR WILLIAM (*pointing at Isabel; triumphantly*) Still in the garden of Eden, madam, still in the Garden of Eden.

(*There is a roll of thunder*)

ISABEL (*moving down* RC) He's just asking for a thunderbolt.

(*There is a terrific clap of thunder and several flashes of lightning.* BARBARA *and* SERENA *scream*)

SIR WILLIAM (*to Joe; with his arm on Joe's shoulder*) Oh, magnificent male!

(JOE *crosses above Sir William and the sofa and stands down* L. BARBARA *gets off the easy chair and stands above it*)

Act II THE BRIDE AND THE BACHELOR 53

Down with the pipe and slipper. Down with the bed and the breakfast. (*He points at Isabel*) Down with the human hot-water bottle.

ISABEL (*calling up to the heavens with her hands cupped round her mouth*) It's not our fault! It's not our fault! Your man's gone mad. (*She sits in the easy chair*)

(SERENA *sits on the right arm of the easy chair*)

SIR WILLIAM (*crossing to* R *of Joe; above the din*) But we are out-numbered. (*He crosses to Jason*) In this, our island home, there are one million seven hundred thousand more women than men.

JASON. Oh, *calamity!*

(BLODWEN *enters by the upstairs archway. She is a weird figure dressed in night attire and sleeping cap, with a cloak thrown over her shoulders. She takes a look at the scene below, then hurries down the stairs*)

SIR WILLIAM. Backs to the wall then, gentlemen. Think of Agincourt! Crecy!
SERENA (*rising*) Joe . . .
SIR WILLIAM. Blenheim! Oudenarde!
BARBARA (*yelling with excitement*) Malplaquet!
SIR WILLIAM (*moving* C) Remember Dunkirk! (*He drinks*)
SERENA (*crossing and kneeling on the sofa at the left end*) Joe, stop him.
JOE (*in awed tones*) It's the greatest thing since Gettysburg.
SERENA (*sinking on to the sofa*) Joe!
JASON (*suddenly transported to Churchillian heights*) We shall fight on the beaches! We shall fight in the homes!
ISABEL (*rising and circling* R *of the easy chair to Jason*) Now, look here, Jason . . .
JASON (*the worm turned*) Sit down!

(ISABEL, *flabbergasted, sits on the right arm of the easy chair*)

JOE (*taking up the battle*) At St Margaret's, Westminster! (*He staggers around near the newel post*)
JASON. And Caxton Hall!
ISABEL (*rising and moving to* L *of Jason*) Wait till I get you upstairs.
JOE. We shall fight upstairs! Downstairs!
JASON (*triumphantly*) And in my lady's *chamber*!
JOE. To the single life—and the battling bachelor. (*He waves his arm*) Hail!
SIR WILLIAM (*raising his glass*) Hail!
JASON (*raising his arm*) Hail!
ISABEL. Jason!

Sir William. Workers of the world, unite! You have nothing to lose but your *wives*.

Jason (*carried away*) Bravo! Bra-bloody-vissimo!

Isabel. How *dare* you! (*She gives Jason a resounding slap across the face*)

The thunder crashes, the wind roars and the lightning flashes. Barbara *dances up and down in a frenzy of excitement.* Joe *passes clean out, at the bottom of the stairs, into* Blodwen's *arms as—*

the Curtain *falls*

ACT III

SCENE—*The same. About nine forty-five a.m., the next morning.*

When the CURTAIN *rises, it is raining and the wind wails outside. A thin watery light filters through the french windows. The room has been tidied, and the coffee table removed. The only sign of the previous night's activities is the bowl, which is still on the floor down* R. BLOD-WEN *is busily engaged,* R *of the easy chair, with a vacuum cleaner. She is in high spirits and is singing "All through the Night" in Welsh.*

BLODWEN (*singing*)
"Ban an nui yewr, Lloin arri an with,
  Ar heed er norse. Ban an nui yewr,
  Lloin arri an with, Ar heed er norse."

(*By this time, her cleaning has taken her to the bowl on the floor down* R. *She picks it up, looks cautiously at it, then puts it on the mantelpiece. She turns the cleaner upstage and continues working and singing*)

"Ban an nui yewr, Lloin arri an with . . ."

(ISABEL *enters by the upstairs archway. Her spirits are low. She wears a pair of dark glasses. She looks cautiously round the room and recoils at the sight of Blodwen so cheerful below. She makes a slow and careful descent of the stairs*)

(*She waves cheerfully*) Bore-da! (*She resumes her lay*)

"Ar heed er norse. Ban an nui yewr,
  Lloin arri an with, Ar heed er norse,
  Vree an gwenny—(*She hits a high note*) ah-ah-aah-ah."

ISABEL (*shouting*) *Blodwen!* I'm not up to the howl of the Hoover today. Do you mind?

(BLODWEN *switches off the cleaner with her foot*)

BLODWEN (*in admiration*) My, but you look tup.
ISABEL (*at the foot of the stairs*) I never felt less tup in my life.
BLODWEN. Is it bad you are in the belly?
ISABEL. No, the brain. I have a splitting headache and I'm trying to concentrate.
BLODWEN. What on?
ISABEL. On—that's the trouble. I'm not quite sure.
BLODWEN (*unplugging the cleaner from a point below the fireplace*) Have some coffee.

(ISABEL *moves to the sofa and lies on it with her head at the left end*)

ISABEL. No, just give me a year or two flat on my back in a darkened room, and I'll be as right as rain.

(*A sudden gust of wind is heard*)

BLODWEN (*moving to the french windows with the cleaner*) Comin' down wet and wonderful, isn't it? (*She turns*) The angels is cryin' their eyes out, as dad used to say.

ISABEL (*putting a hand to her head*) Dad must have been psychic.

BLODWEN. Try the coffee. It quickens the spirits, makes the heart lightsome and closes the orifice of the stomach.

ISABEL (*with a hand to her midriff*) Don't!

BLODWEN. Good also it is against coughs, colds, consumption, gout and King's Evil.

(*There is a gust of wind.* ISABEL *sits up and removes her glasses.*
BLODWEN *exits up* R *with the cleaner and re-enters immediately with a duster. Humming, she moves* R *of the easy chair and plumps and tidies the cushions. The wind fades*)

ISABEL (*nervously*) Blodwen, when you got up this morning and came in here, you didn't by any chance happen to notice, did you, if there was—that is, there—there wasn't any sign, was there, of—what I'm trying to say is—(*in a rush*) last night's sandwiches weren't as fresh as they might have been, were they?

BLODWEN (*miffed*) Sandwiches?

ISABEL (*rising and standing* R *of the sofa; hastily*) Oh, please don't think I'm complaining. No, no. I'm delighted. The more disgusting they were the better. You see, I had the most extraordinary dream in the night and—well, the sandwiches would account for it. Of course, I knew all the time I was dreaming. Oh, yes, I'm not a complete fool. I said to myself at regular intervals, "It's all right. I'm dreaming—I'm dreaming. In the cold light of day this—this apparition will vanish into thin air——

(SIR WILLIAM *enters by the upstairs archway and comes slowly down the stairs.* ISABEL *does not immediately see him*)

—and I shall stand around laughing madly at the whole thing." I suppose if one has more imagination than most, one just has to pay for it. Never mind, I'm awake now and I'm going to start laughing immediately. Here I go, ha, ha, ha, ha, ha—ccccchk. (*The laugh segues into a violent attack of coughing as she sees Sir William. She hastily puts on her dark glasses*)

(SIR WILLIAM, *unmoved, picks up a copy of "The Times" from the left arm of the sofa, crosses and exits down* R. BLODWEN *follows Sir William down* R)

BLODWEN (*calling affably after Sir William*) Have a nice breakfast, ghostie. I got a fine fire goin' for you. (*She closes the door and*

ACT III THE BRIDE AND THE BACHELOR 57

turns to Isabel. Sympathetically) It must be hard to get warm when you got rigor mortis, isn't it? (*She dusts the mantelpiece*)

ISABEL (*removing her glasses and sitting on the sofa*) I'll be in a position to tell you for sure very shortly.

BLODWEN (*crossing above the easy chair to* C) Oh, I known he was one of them soon as I set eyes on him. I says to him, "Ghostie, I seen your picture in the paper, large as life, so I known you was dead," I says. (*She pauses*) Regardin' the notice . . .

ISABEL (*a nervous wreck*) Yes, yes—I understand—you'll be leaving at once. I shall be right behind you.

BLODWEN (*astonished*) On account of poor ghostie? (*She crosses to the stairs and dusts the banisters*) We think nothing o' them in the Valley. Old Uncle Dai Evans, the Coal, who hung on till a hundred and three—(*she leans over the banisters*) "Never-say-Dai", he was known as—ha, ha—he comes back every Christmas to wish us the compliments and to see what he's got in his stocking. (*She works up the stairs*)

(ISABEL *reaches over the back of the sofa, picks up the indexed telephone pad from the table above the sofa, and looks up a number*)

Well, it's friendly like, isn't it? (*She leans over the banisters at the turn of the stairs*) Regardin' the notice—(*she dusts along the balcony rail*) I thought it all over and so long as you don't get too happy, I'm happy to stay.

(BLODWEN *exits by the upstairs archway.* ISABEL *rises, hurries to the door down* R, *listens a moment, then crosses rapidly to the telephone, lifts the receiver and dials a number*)

WOMAN'S VOICE (*off; through the telephone; young and hearty*) Hullo-o . . .

ISABEL (*into the telephone; keeping her voice low, and with one eye on the door down* R) Hullo, is that the Vicarage?

(BARBARA *enters down* R *and moves above the easy chair. She carries a copy of the "Daily Mail"*)

WOMAN'S VOICE. St John's here. What can we do for you?

ISABEL (*urgently*) This is Mrs Kilpatrick. I want to speak to the Vicar.

BARBARA. Mother.

(ISABEL *slams down the receiver*)

What do you want the Vicar for? (*She sits on the left arm of the easy chair*)

ISABEL (*airily*) Never you mind.

BARBARA (*suspiciously*) Why were you phoning the Vicar?

ISABEL (*moving and picking up a copy of the "Tatler" from the right arm of the sofa*) I said, "Never mind." (*She moves down* L *of the sofa*)

BARBARA (*suddenly*) You want to get rid of him.

ISABEL (*continuing round the sofa to up* L *of it*) Don't be absurd. He's an excellent Vicar. Mumbles, of course, but then, most of them mumble.

BARBARA (*rising and pointing to the door down* R) Him! (*Accusingly*) You want to have him exorcised. You do!

ISABEL (*moving* C; *defiantly*) Yes, I do. And at the first conceivable moment, if such a thing's possible in this year of grace.

BARBARA. Of all the rotten tricks. Exorcism's for evil spirits. Willie's not evil.

(*The sound of the wind is heard*)

ISABEL. So it's "Willie" now. Charming.

BARBARA (*moving below the easy chair and sitting on the right arm of it*) We chummed up over breakfast. (*She looks towards the door down* R) He's not at all a bad sort of ghost, as ghosts go.

ISABEL. But as ghosts go, he doesn't.

BARBARA. He can't. I'm real sorry for Willie.

ISABEL (*boiling*) You can go on being sorry for him till you're blue in the face—so far as I'm concerned, he's had it.

(*A big gust of wind interrupts her*)

(*She moves up* C) Look at the weather. What's the forecast?

BARBARA (*referring to her newspaper*) "Dry and sunny." But the Stop Press says, "Freak storm hits North London. Weather men baffled."

ISABEL (*moving down* C) Why baffled? We're obviously going to be wiped out like Tyre and Nineveh. Oh, well, there's one amongst us who'll enjoy every minute of it.

BARBARA. Who?

ISABEL (*sitting on the sofa*) Willie. Manchester weather does something for him. We'd better lock Blodwen in the attic.

(SIR WILLIAM *enters down* R. *He carries the copy of "The Times" which he puts on the right arm of the sofa*)

SIR WILLIAM. Oh—good morning. I just wanted to return *The Times*.

ISABEL (*icily*) Would you care for the *Tatler*?

SIR WILLIAM. Er—thank you—no. (*He moves to the french windows and gazes out*) Not much of a day.

ISABEL. As a description of the worst downpour since Noah, that rather lacks bite, don't you feel?

SIR WILLIAM (*moving* C) Is something the matter?

ISABEL (*bitterly*) Ha!

(*The wind fades*)

SIR WILLIAM. I went a bit far last night.

Act III   THE BRIDE AND THE BACHELOR

ISABEL (*moving along the sofa seat to the left end and looking* L) Far? Far?

SIR WILLIAM (*sitting on the sofa at the right end*) That speech was rather inviting the fates, in the circumstances. It was part of my Presidential address at the Bachelors' Club. The half that was undelivered owing to my sudden demise. The shock of meeting my daughter must have touched off a reflex and impelled me to go into action. I take it I did so—with some force.

ISABEL. As you can hardly have failed to hear, you went over with a bang. The Club now has two new members, including *my husband.*

SIR WILLIAM. Curious. It's quite gone from me this morning.

ISABEL. Too bad you didn't go with it.

SIR WILLIAM. You know, I, myself, am the principal victim of my defection. I appear to be permanently grounded.

ISABEL (*coldly*) In that case you'll have to look for lodgings elsewhere. You can't stop on here. Go to an hotel. Take a suite at the *Dorchester.*

(BARBARA *rises, moves down* R, *puts the newspaper on the stool, then sits on the floor by the stool*)

BARBARA. He'd never get in. It's the Motor Show.

ISABEL (*exasperated*) Then try a hospital—or a nursing home. What's that one the Bulstrode girl keeps popping in and out of in Welbeck Street?

BARBARA. That's for when you're going to become a mother.

ISABEL. Well, he's just become a father. Maybe they'd stretch a point.

(BARBARA *picks up her paper, sprawls on the floor and reads.*

JASON *enters by the upstairs archway. He is in morning clothes, and comes down the stairs polishing his glasses. Without his glasses he is unable to see Sir William*)

SIR WILLIAM (*rising*) Madam, once and for all, and bitterly though we both may regret it, I am unable to dwell anywhere on earth except in this house. (*He picks up "The Times", moves to the armchair up* R, *sits and reads*)

ISABEL. In that case, *I* shall go to Welbeck Street. I will not share my home with a spectre.

(SIR WILLIAM, *reading, is oblivious*)

JASON (*at the foot of the stairs; cheerfully*) Good morning, my dear.

ISABEL. Two spectres.

JASON (*moving to* L *of the sofa and admiring Isabel's dress*) I say, what a ripping rig-out.

ISABEL. Flattery will get you nowhere.

JASON (*crossing above the sofa to* C) Not much of a morning for the ceremony. Quite overcast. Never mind, perhaps it will perk up later. (*He moves to* R *of the table above the sofa*) It—it is morning, isn't it?

ISABEL. It makes no odds.

JASON. The reason I ask is a dream I had in the night. (*He breathes on the lenses and continues to polish his glasses*) I dreamed I heard voices, and came down here in my pyjamas, and you were here with Serena and Babs, and some chap who was dead. Not at all a bad fellow, with some rather amusing ideas about women and so forth. And then you slapped my face and I . . . (*He turns* R, *puts on his glasses and sees Sir William*) Well, I'm blessed! (*He turns to Isabel*) I must have dropped off again.

ISABEL. Will someone inform my ex-husband that in so far as he *can* be conscious, he is.

JASON (*amazed*) You mean, I'm awake all the time?

ISABEL. I didn't say *that*, did I?

JASON (*moving below the pillar* RC; *to Sir William*) "We'll fight on the beaches, we'll fight in the homes . . ." I really *did* say that?

SIR WILLIAM. I'm afraid so.

JASON (*eyeing Isabel; nervously*) Well, but, in that case, I must have . . .

BARBARA (*sitting up*) You did! You did! It was wonderful.

(JASON, *realizing that something is called for, moves to* R *of the sofa*)

JASON (*tentatively*) Er—Isabel, my dear . . .

ISABEL. I think it would be as well if we communicated through our solicitors until after the divorce. (*She eyes Barbara darkly*) Incidentally, I shall not be claiming custody of the child.

JASON (*sitting* R *of Isabel on the sofa, taking her hand and patting it*) Oh, come now. "For better, for worse, for richer, for poorer . . ."

BARBARA. ". . . To love and to cherish, till death do us part."

ISABEL (*with a gesture towards Sir William*) It has—the lot of us. What's more, if the Vicar can't help us, he's with us for life. (*She throws Jason's hand off*)

JASON. Who? The Vicar?

ISABEL (*exasperated*) No, not the Vicar.

BARBARA. She wants him to exorcise Willie.

JASON. Willie? Willie? What Willie?

ISABEL (*nodding up* R *and pointing*) Willie.

BARBARA. If it worked, he'd go under for ever. We must get him back up.

JASON. Ah, yes. Indeed, yes. By all means.

ISABEL. By what means?

JASON (*rising and moving below the pillar* RC) Well, I really don't know. I suppose he couldn't—(*he mimes a "take off"*) just take off spontaneously.

ACT III THE BRIDE AND THE BACHELOR

ISABEL. I'll ask him. (*To Sir William*) Could you take off spontaneously?

SIR WILLIAM (*emerging from behind "The Times"*) My dear good lady, the voluntary levitationist, if and when his time comes, will presumably require at least a grounding in astrophysics. I ran a Department Store. (*He goes back to his paper*)

JASON. Yes, of course. Swan and Edgars.

ISABEL. We're wasting time. (*To Jason*) Go round to the Vicar. Tell him the wedding's off. We want an exorcism instead.

JASON. Exorcism? Wetherby-Wilkes is a splendid fellow, but I fear this will be beyond him. (*He backs up* RC *into the pillar*) I beg your pardon. (*He turns and realizes*) Oh, confound the thing!

(JASON *exits up* R)

BARBARA. D'you mean Serena's not going to be married?

ISABEL. How *can* she be married? The bridegroom's gone over to the enemy.

(JOE *enters by the upstairs archway. He appears to be suffering from a hangover.* SIR WILLIAM *rises and moves up* C)

BLODWEN (*off upstairs*) Easy, Joe bach, easy. We don't want to break nothing.

JOE (C *of the balcony*) Momsy.

(BLODWEN *enters by the upstairs archway*)

BLODWEN. All right, bach?

JOE (*turning and taking Blodwen's hands*) Oh, yeah. Thanks, honey. Thanks a million—for everything. The—the bed and— and everything. (*He moves halfway down the stairs*)

(BARBARA *and* ISABEL *stare at Blodwen*)

BLODWEN. The pleasure was all mine, isn't it? (*She becomes aware of the stares*)

(ISABEL *looks hard at Blodwen*)

(*Sharply*) Think not wicked thoughts. The couch in the corridor did me fine. I sublimated.

(BLODWEN *exits by the upstairs archway*)

JOE (*stumbling down the stairs and squatting* L *of the sofa*) Momsy, I—I want to apologize. Last night—I seem to recall I . . . (*He struggles to his feet*)

ISABEL (*moving with a half rise to the right end of the sofa seat*) I think you'd apologize better sitting down, Joe.

(SIR WILLIAM *moves to the easy chair and sits*)

JOE. Thanks, I—I don't feel so good. (*He sits* L *of Isabel on the sofa*) Say, he doesn't look too hot, either.

ISABEL. He's not.

JOE. Is sugar-plum up?

BARBARA. She was snoring like twenty mule-trains when I came down.

JOE. Could you go wake her, Barbie? Tell her—tell her Joe says, "Rise and shine, you'll be late for *Lohengrin*."

BARBARA (*rising*) You mean we're back in business? Zowie! (*She runs to the stairs and goes up them, singing "The Wedding March" at the top of her voice*)

(BARBARA *exits by the upstairs archway*)

ISABEL. If I suddenly start to shriek, forgive me, won't you?

SIR WILLIAM (*to Joe*) Are we to infer from that message that you wish to re-enter the market?

JOE (*politely*) Come again?

SIR WILLIAM (*loudly*) Do you now wish to marry my daughter, sir?

JOE (*rising*) I always have wanted to marry her, sir. From the very first moment I met her, right there in the desert.

SIR WILLIAM. The desert?

ISABEL. The Arabian desert. He was out there with Nescaf.

JOE (*leaning on the banisters*) UNESCO.

(ISABEL *looks puzzled, then beams recognition*)

We were in a spot we called "Hole-In-The-Head". There were three of us. We were buddies.

SIR WILLIAM. Three?

JOE. Yep. Simon and Scotty and me. (*He slaps his stomach and groans*) Boy, I feel terrible.

ISABEL (*rising*) Sit down and take a deep breath.

JOE (*sitting on the sofa at the left end*) So—there we are—at night—in the desert, with nothing but baked beans and a package of Murray-Mints.

(ISABEL *crosses above the sofa to* L *of it*)

When who should come over the horizon but a girl—and a character on a camel.

SIR WILLIAM. What kind of character?

ISABEL. My husband. Sheik Gluk had invited him to the outer oases and Serena went with him to sugar the pill.

JOE (*rising and moving* C) Well, sir, imagine—three guys in a hole like Hole-In-The-Head—and then, all of a sudden, this girl on this camel. The girl was so goddam beautiful, and the camel was so goddam ugly . . .

ISABEL. He fell in love rightaway. With the girl, not the camel.

JOE. I just sort of stood there and gaped, sir.

(ISABEL *sits on the sofa at the right end*)

ACT III THE BRIDE AND THE BACHELOR

And then all of a sudden she smiled—and offered us a cup of tea from her water-bottle. That did it! (*He slaps his knee and sits on the right arm of the sofa*)

SIR WILLIAM. Did what?

ISABEL (*romantically*) He fell in love, of course. And for three whole days those three boys pitched their tents alongside Serena's. Oh, it couldn't have been more romantic.

JOE. I dreamed about her all night long. I saw her back in Omaha with mom, in the all-electric kitchen, helping mom with her blueberry pie. She was *woman—all woman*.

ISABEL. She could hardly have been anything else. What I mean is, I never quite know what that means.

JOE (*springing to his feet; to Isabel*) It means there's a lot to be said for the single life, but—(*to Sir William*) boy, you can *make mine marriage*.

(SERENA *enters dreamily by the upstage archway and drifts to the left end of the balcony*)

(*He moves up* R *of the sofa and points at Serena*) I, Joseph, take thee, Serena, to my lawful wedded wife.

ISABEL (*rising and crossing to* R *of Joe*) Home and dry!

JOE. To have and to hold from this day forward, for better and for worse.

SERENA (*leaning over the balcony; trance-like*) You're very sweet, Joseph—and very young. (*She comes halfway down the stairs*) Goodbye, my dear.

JOE (*puzzled*) I'm not goin' any place.

(ISABEL *looks bewildered*)

SERENA (*with the calmness of a saint*) But I am. (*She looks at Sir William*) I'm going—where father's come from.

(ISABEL *sinks on to the left arm of the easy chair*)

JOE (*baffled*) Australia?

(SIR WILLIAM *rises, throws up his hands and moves to the fireplace*)

SERENA. And then we can be together for ever and ever.

ISABEL (*rising and moving below the sofa*) Now look here, Serena. If you want to be married, you shall. If you don't want to marry, you shan't. But I will not tell the guests there's to be no wedding, but to stand by for a *Wake*.

(*There is a pause.* SERENA *crosses and stands below the easy chair*)

SERENA. I'm so unhappy.
ISABEL. Serena!
SERENA. And it's all your fault.
ISABEL (*taken aback*) My fault?

SERENA (*with a step towards Isabel*) For getting him here in the first place.

ISABEL. But it was an accident. (*She takes a step towards Serena*) I wouldn't make you unhappy for anything in the world.

SERENA (*turning away*) Don't say any more—please. (*She turns to Isabel*) You've ruined my life with your silly spells. Isn't that enough?

(SERENA, *on the verge of tears, goes off down* R)

JOE (*crossing to the door down* R) Is she kangaroo crazy or sump'n?

(JOE *exits down* R)

SIR WILLIAM (*with a step towards Isabel*) This is all very distressing, and I must say I feel largely responsible.

(ISABEL *suddenly sits on the sofa and starts to cry quietly*)

(*He is acutely embarrassed and genuinely concerned*) My dear Mrs Kilpatrick—(*he moves below the easy chair*)

(ISABEL *sobs*)

—is there anything *I* can do?

ISABEL (*choked*) Yes, but . . .

SIR WILLIAM (*moving to* R *of the sofa*) You have only to ask.

ISABEL. You—you don't know how. (*She blows her nose*)

SIR WILLIAM (*at a loss*) How?

ISABEL (*through her tears*) Astro-physics—you—you never took astro-physics. (*She sobs*)

SIR WILLIAM. I was, I confess, a classical man, and I've never had much head for heights—I was lost on the top of Beachy Head as a child—however, if you think it will do any good, I'll —I'll try. (*He gallantly tries a little voluntary levitation. He rises on his toes, half-turned away to* R, *with arms outstretched, and bounces upwards and forwards on his toes. Having no success, he does a little run down* R *and bobs upwards again several times, but still fails to take wing. He moves above the easy chair; a little breathless*) I'm afraid it's hopeless.

ISABEL. Thank you for trying.

SIR WILLIAM (*moving up* C) Not at all. I lack the gift completely.

(*The wind starts gently*)

ISABEL (*suddenly; staring ahead of her*) Gift . . .

SIR WILLIAM (*moving* C) Can I get you some coffee?

ISABEL. No—no, I—yes. Yes, I would like some coffee.

(SIR WILLIAM *exits up* R. *The moment she is alone,* ISABEL *rises, moves up* R, *looks off, moves* C, *looks around to make sure she is unobserved, then goes to the mantelpiece and picks up the bowl. She goes*

ACT III THE BRIDE AND THE BACHELOR

to the french windows and holds up the bowl. The wind comes in a great gust, so she turns, comes slowly down below the easy chair, faces front and nervously holds up the bowl)

(*Shyly*) It's me again. I'm so very sorry to bother you, I expect you're frightfully busy. I know it's not midnight—and—and there's no moon—and—and we've had our quota, but—well, we've got ourselves in the most awful mess. So if—if you could possibly help—what I mean is——

(BARBARA *enters by the upstairs archway. She is dressed in her bridesmaid's outfit. Unseen by* ISABEL, *she moves* C *of the balcony and watches*)

—(*from her heart; with desperate sincerity*) oh, "Quel atranta, quel atronta, quel atronta, quel atrine." Oh, please, *please*, PLEASE!

(*The wind dies softly away*)

BARBARA (*at length; admiringly*) At it again?

(ISABEL *swings violently round*)

Good old Mum!

ISABEL (*caught in the act*) Don't you *dare* tell! (*She puts the bowl under the cushion on the easy chair*)

BARBARA. Guess that's how you get your kicks, huh?

ISABEL (*moving up* R) That does it! Where's the *Bradshaw*?

BARBARA (*coming down the stairs*) What did I do now?

ISABEL (*moving down* RC; *furiously*) Tunbridge Wells to you. Tunbridge Wells.

BARBARA (*running to* L *of Isabel*) Look, you don't have to put me away. I won't tell.

ISABEL. One word to a living soul . . .

BARBARA (*putting her arms around Isabel; wheedling*) Don't you trust me?

ISABEL. Like a boa-constrictor.

BARBARA. You can. Honest!

ISABEL. *Swear.*

BARBARA. Guide's Honour, George Washington, cross my heart.

ISABEL (*pushing Barbara away* L) Get out of that outfit immediately.

BARBARA. I thought the wedding was on.

ISABEL. It's off again.

BARBARA (*crossing to the stairs*) Hells' bells. (*She goes slowly up the stairs*)

(MISS BOWDEN, *dressed as in Act I, enters up* R, *and crosses to* R *of the sofa. She carries a wet umbrella and her handbag*)

ISABEL. Don't swear.

BARBARA (*halfway up the stairs*) You just told me to.
ISABEL (*suddenly seeing Miss Bowden*) And who's this?
BARBARA (*over the balcony*) Barlow and Morrison's—to see her into it.

(BARBARA *exits by the upstairs archway*)

ISABEL. See who into what? Oh, the wedding gown. Yes, well, it'll have to go back.

(SIR WILLIAM *enters up* R *and moves to* R *of Isabel. He carries a cup of coffee.* MISS BOWDEN *gazes raptly at Sir William*)

We may shortly be needing a shroud, but I expect that's a different department. (*She takes the coffee from Sir William*) Thank you.

(SIR WILLIAM *moves to the fireplace and looks at the invitations on the mantelpiece*)

(*She sits on the right arm of the easy chair and mutters to herself*) Barlow and Morrison's. (*She goes to sip the coffee, realizes, stops suddenly, rises, edges to* L *of Sir William and speaks close to his ear*) Barlow and Morrison's.

SIR WILLIAM (*turning*) I beg your pardon?

ISABEL (*handing the coffee to Sir William; giving up*) You'll want this more than I shall. (*She moves to the door down* R. *To Miss Bowden*) What goes up must come down.

(ISABEL *exits rapidly down* R)

MISS BOWDEN (*quite still*) You're Sir William Barlow, aren't you? I'm from the Store.

SIR WILLIAM (*moving to* R *of the easy chair*) Oh, yes? I'm afraid I don't know you.

MISS BOWDEN (*quietly*) Don't you, Will?

(SIR WILLIAM *stares at her*)

(*She grins broadly*) Time's marched on a bit since Manchester—but—(*she moves down* R *of the sofa*) the rain's no different, eh, lad? (*She shakes the umbrella*)

SIR WILLIAM. My God! Nellie! (*He all but drops the coffee*)

MISS BOWDEN (*chuckling*) Aye.

SIR WILLIAM. How—how are you, my dear?

MISS BOWDEN. Grand, love, thanks. (*She holds out her hand*) How's yourself?

SIR WILLIAM (*moving to* R *of Miss Bowden and shaking hands*) I'm—well. That is—I take it—you've not seen the papers?

MISS BOWDEN. You mean, about you and Kingdom Come? Oh, I know all about that. (*She turns away* L)

SIR WILLIAM (*astonished*) You—you do? And you're not—frightened?

ACT III THE BRIDE AND THE BACHELOR 67

MISS BOWDEN (*turning to him; laughing*) Frightened? At seein' my Will? Why should I be frightened?
SIR WILLIAM. I'm—glad you take it this way.
MISS BOWDEN. How did you expect me to take it? There are more things in heaven and earth, eh, lad?
SIR WILLIAM (*almost sitting on the right arm of the easy chair*) Indeed—indeed. (*He straightens up, feeling some social advance is indicated*) Er—would you care for some coffee?
MISS BOWDEN (*taking the coffee from him*) I don't mind if I do. Thanks very much. (*She sits on the sofa at the right end*) Well, this is nice. Our lass is a beauty, isn't she? (*She sips the coffee*)
SIR WILLIAM (*moving to R of the sofa; in amazement*) Our . . .? You know all about that, too?
MISS BOWDEN. Why do you think I'm here? I kept track of her all her life, bless her.
SIR WILLIAM (*suddenly; seeking refuge in anger*) Then why did you give her up? You—you abandoned her on a public doorstep. Didn't you want your own child?
· MISS BOWDEN (*rising, moving round L of the sofa and putting the cup on the table above the sofa*) Now don't get yourself in a lather. Sit down. I won't bite.

(SIR WILLIAM *sits on the sofa at the right end*)

That's better. (*She sits L of Sir William on the sofa*) 'Course I wanted her. But I wanted the best for her, and I thought that was you. When I saw in the papers what a muck-up I'd made I longed to have her back. But I couldn't have her without telling on you, and that would have put the cat among the canaries proper like, wouldn't it? So—well, they were decent folk with a decent home, from all accounts . . .
SIR WILLIAM (*sincerely*) You're a grand girl, Nellie.
MISS BOWDEN (*taking a handkerchief from her bag and blowing her nose*) Not so bad yourself—I followed your career, you know.
SIR WILLIAM. Really?
MISS BOWDEN. Kept all your cuttings and such like. Daft, wasn't I?
SIR WILLIAM. Oh, I don't know.
MISS BOWDEN. I was waiting for you to latch on to some lass and settle down, see. But when you didn't, I said to myself, "Nay, our Will's as scared as ever."
SIR WILLIAM (*annoyed*) Scared? Scared of what?
MISS BOWDEN. Marriage, love. Scared to death of it, weren't you?
SIR WILLIAM. Nonsense! It was a matter of principle.
MISS BOWDEN. And now it's got into our girl. Cold feet must be catching. (*She rises and moves to the foot of the stairs*) Oh, well, you'll soon put her to rights. (*She starts up the stairs*)
SIR WILLIAM. Put her to rights?

MISS BOWDEN (*leaning over the banisters*) Tell her you won't have her make the same muck-up you did. Tell her to go and get hitched and no argument.

SIR WILLIAM (*raising his voice*) I shall do no such thing.

MISS BOWDEN. And don't shout. Just tell her nice and quiet, there's a good lad.

SIR WILLIAM (*rising*) I shall do nothing of the kind.

MISS BOWDEN (*commandingly*) Easy, lad, easy. (*She comes down the stairs, crosses to* L *of Sir William and puts her right hand on his shoulder*) It's me—Nellie—remember? Now, go on, love. Be a good boy.

SIR WILLIAM (*turning away* R; *mumbling*) She—she'd never believe me.

MISS BOWDEN (*quietly*) 'Appen you're the only one she would believe. 'Appen that's why you're here, eh, lad? (*She glances at her watch*) Only you'll have to get cracking, she's due at the church in twelve minutes. (*She crosses to the stairs*) I'll have the dress ready. (*She starts up the stairs*)

SIR WILLIAM (*suddenly panicking*) Don't leave me! Don't leave me!

MISS BOWDEN (*pausing on the stairs*) I'm only upstairs. Oh, she's had shock enough finding her dad. Best not let on about her ma. Mum's the word, eh, love? (*She goes up the stairs and on to the balcony*)

(SIR WILLIAM *sits on the right arm of the sofa. The door down* R *opens.*

SERENA, ISABEL *and* JOE *sweep in down* R *and cross to* C)

SERENA (*as she enters*) I've made up my mind and nobody's going to unmake it.

(SERENA's *voice halts* MISS BOWDEN *in her progress along the balcony, and she stops by the upstairs archway and looks down. This is the first time she has seen her daughter in the flesh and she is proud and happy*)

ISABEL⎫ (*together*) ⎧Serena, once and for all . . .
JOE ⎭   ⎩Honey, this is the craziest . . .

SERENA (*moving up* C; *her hands over her ears*) Please! Please! Go away. (*To Sir William*) Tell them to go.

ISABEL. Sir William . . .

SIR WILLIAM (*rising; with immense authority*) Out!

ISABEL (*astounded*) I *beg* your pardon?

SIR WILLIAM (*more quietly*) No. I beg yours. But, out—please.

(ISABEL *hesitates*)

ISABEL (*helplessly*) Well, *really*! (*To Joe*) Out!

(ISABEL *exits down* R.

ACT III THE BRIDE AND THE BACHELOR

(JOE *follows her off, throwing a backward, puzzled glare as he goes*)

SIR WILLIAM (*sitting on the sofa at the left end*) Come here.

(SERENA *sits* R *of Sir William on the sofa*)

How old are you?
SERENA. Twenty-one.

(MISS BOWDEN *beams and nods*)

SIR WILLIAM. Yes, that's right. And your birthday must be—somewhere in March——

(MISS BOWDEN *shakes her head in disagreement*)

—no, April.

(MISS BOWDEN *nods her agreement*)

SERENA. April the first. No cracks.
SIR WILLIAM. I wish I'd been there—at the beginning.
SERENA. Never mind, you're here at the end.

(MISS BOWDEN *slips out by the upstairs archway*)

(*She looks upwards*) What's it like up there?
SIR WILLIAM. I wish I'd been—all the way with you. Childhood—school—and when you began to feel frightened.
SERENA. Frightened! What of?
SIR WILLIAM. Marriage.
SERENA (*turning away* R; *startled*) I—I'm not frightened of marriage—I . . .
SIR WILLIAM. You get it from me, you know, as I got it from *my* father. I was scared to death, too—and I wouldn't admit it, either.
SERENA (*turning to him*) But I—I'm not scared. You mean, *that's* why I keep on dreaming?
SIR WILLIAM (*nodding*) Excuses. Subconscious excuses.
SERENA (*rising*) It—it can't be. (*She moves* R *of the sofa*) I'm not scared. I'll show you I'm not.
SIR WILLIAM. Show me.
SERENA (*after a pause*) Oh, I see. It's a bamboozle. You're trying to trap me into it.
SIR WILLIAM. Excuses again.
SERENA (*bewildered*) But I don't understand. You—you're not just saying this because you want to go back—(*she looks upwards*) up there?
SIR WILLIAM. No. I'm saying it because I want you to stay—down here.
SERENA (*sitting* R *of Sir William on the sofa and staring at him*) Cross your heart and hope to . . .?

SIR WILLIAM (*putting out his hand for hers; sincerely*) And hope most prayerfully, once and for all, to ...

(SERENA *puts her arms around Sir William and leans her head on his shoulder*)

SERENA. Perhaps if I went to sleep again——

(SIR WILLIAM *slips his arm around her*)

—perhaps one more dream ...
SIR WILLIAM (*softly*) Serena. Take a leap in the dark, with your eyes wide open. That's marriage.

(SERENA *leans away to look up at him, then returns her head to his shoulder. The telephone rings.*
ISABEL *enters down* R *and crosses to the telephone*)

ISABEL. Excuse me—(*she lifts the receiver*) that must be the Vicar. (*Into the telephone*) Hallo?
OPERATOR (*off; through the telephone*) Long Distance is calling you.
ISABEL. Long distance? Who on earth can be calling long distance?

(*Crackling sounds come from the receiver*)

There's a most peculiar crackling noise——

(*Swishing sounds are now heard*)

—and a blasting of wind, as if ...

(*A blowing sound like a maroon interrupts her*)

My God!
MALE VOICE (*off; through the telephone*) Hullo? Hullo there?
ISABEL (*into the telephone; faintly*) Hallo? W-who are you?
MALE VOICE. Can you hear me?
ISABEL. Yes. I can hear you. *Who are you?*
MALE VOICE. This is—Peter.
ISABEL. *Peter!* P— Peter who?
MALE VOICE. Peter Washington Tilney.
ISABEL (*with profound relief*) Peter Washington Tilney. It's Joe's father. (*Into the telephone*) Oh, I'm so sorry, Mr Tilney. (*She calls*) Joe. (*Into the telephone*) For a moment I thought it was someone else.
MALE VOICE. Is my boy with you?

(JOE *enters down* R)

ISABEL. Yes, yes, he's just coming. (*To Joe*) It's for you.
JOE. Huh?
ISABEL (*putting the receiver on the table*) Your father.

ACT III THE BRIDE AND THE BACHELOR 71

(ISABEL *hurries out up* R, *murmuring* "*Oh, I will give you the keys of heaven!*" JOE *crosses to the telephone and picks up the receiver*)

JOE (*into the telephone*) Hi, Dad!
MALE VOICE. I called your hotel, boy, but they said you'd been out all night. What goes on?
JOE. Well, see, Dad, there's been kind of a change of plan. Kinda looks like I'm not going to be married after all.

(SIR WILLIAM *straightens* SERENA *up and holds her eyes with his*)

MALE VOICE. How's that again?

(SERENA *looks down, then up at Sir William and smiles*)

JOE. I said I guess the wedding's off. You see, the Turkish Embassy . . .
MALE VOICE. Are you sick, boy?
JOE (*floundering*) Look, Dad—her father in Portland Place—he's an Australian . . .

(SERENA *kisses Sir William, then rises and moves* R *of the sofa*)

MALE VOICE (*getting mad*) I don't understand a goddam word you're saying.

(SERENA *crosses in front of Joe to* L *of him and takes the receiver from him*)

SERENA (*into the telephone*) Hullo, Mr Tilney. This is Serena.
MALE VOICE. Well, hullo there, honey. How are you?
SERENA. I'm fine. How are you?
MALE VOICE. Say, what's with that boy of mine?
SERENA. Joe? He's fine, too. (*She rests her head on Joe's shoulder*)
MALE VOICE. He just told me the deal's off.
SERENA. Oh, I don't think he could have said that, Mr Tilney. It must be the line.
MALE VOICE. You mean, you *are* gonna be married?
SERENA. Well, of course we're going to be married. That is, if Joe still . . . Hold on a second. (*To Joe*) Do you still want to marry me, Joe?

(JOE, *amazed, breaks* R)

Well, come on, make up your mind.
JOE (*exploding*) Make up *my* mind. Hell, look who's talking.
SERENA. Joe!
JOE (*moving to Serena; quickly*) Sure, sure I want to be married. I've never wanted to be married so much in all my . . . (*He grabs the receiver in his right hand and puts his left arm around Serena. Into the telephone*) Hullo, Dad? Say, how does the world look to you today? Did you ever see such a wonderful, beautiful place?
MALE VOICE. Then it's all O.K.?

Joe. Bet your life it's okay. Good-bye, Dad.
Serena (*into the telephone*) Good-bye, Dad.

(Joe *replaces the receiver, then takes Serena in his arms*)

Joe. Are you really my girl?
Serena (*joyfully*) I'm really your girl, Joe—if you'll have me. (*She throws her arms around him*)

(Sir William *sits up, smiling.*
   Isabel *enters up* R *and stands by the pillar* RC)

Joe (*hugging Serena; jubilantly*) If I'll have you! See you in church in—(*he looks at his wrist-watch*) eight minutes.

(Joe *rushes off up* R. Isabel *circles the pillar, dodging Joe*)

Isabel. Eight minutes! Where's my hat, where's my hat? (*She looks* C, *then crosses down* L)
Serena (*moving to the stairs*) Oh, heaven!

(Serena *runs up the stairs and exits by the upstairs archway.*
   Isabel *starts to follow her.*
   Jason *enters up* R *and crosses to* C)

Jason. Splendid news! The Vicar's getting in touch with the Archbishop of Canterbury.
Isabel (*leaning over the banisters*) Tell him to get out of touch.

(Barbara *enters by the upstairs archway. She is dressed once more in sweater and jeans*)

Barbara. Well, I'm out of it.
Isabel (*moving on to the balcony*) Get back into it immediately.
Barbara. But you said it was off.
Isabel. Don't argue.

(Isabel *bustles* Barbara *bodily off by the upstairs archway and follows her off*)

Jason. Well, I'm blessed!
Sir William (*dryly*) That remains to be seen.

(*The telephone rings.* Jason *moves to the telephone and lifts the receiver*)

Jason (*into the telephone*) Hullo, hullo, Kilpatrick here.
Male Voice (*off; through the telephone*) That you, Jason?
Jason (*delighted*) Hullo, Proudfoot, old fellow, how are we today?
Voice (*high pitched, gabbling and hysterical*) Disaster—Kuala Lumpur—*Quentin Durward* not dropped jungle—Nyasaland—medical posters dropped—not *Durward*. Disaster, Jason, disaster.

ACT III THE BRIDE AND THE BACHELOR 73

JASON. What? Yes, indeed it *is* a disaster.
VOICE (*wailing*) Jason, what shall we do?
JASON. Oh, well, no good crying over spilt milk, I suppose.
VOICE. I thought I'd better let you know.
JASON. Yes, thank you for the information. Good-bye, old fellow. Chin up. (*He replaces the receiver*)
SIR WILLIAM. Is something the matter?
JASON (*moving below the easy chair*) There's been a most unfortunate contretemps at Kuala Lumpur. The Council had arranged for some copies of *Quentin Durward* to be parachuted into the Malayan jungle, to give the Commies some notion of British chivalry. It seems a cargo of medical posters was dropped in error. (*He sits, a worried man, in the easy chair*)
SIR WILLIAM. What did the posters say?
JASON. "Now is the time to have your chest X-rayed." (*He throws up his hands in despair*)

(ISABEL *enters by the upstairs archway. She has added a matching, fur-collared jacket to her dress, wears her hat, and carries matching handbag and gloves. She looks charming*)

ISABEL. She won't be a minute. (*She hurries down the stairs*)

(JASON *rises*. SIR WILLIAM *looks up*)

Sir William, you'll come to the church and sit on the bride's side, next to me.
JASON (*moving to* R *of the sofa*) Would you care to give her away, my dear fellow?
ISABEL. I hardly think that would be suitable. Sir William's given away quite enough already.
JASON (*to Sir William*) Well, so long as you don't object.
SIR WILLIAM (*rising*) On the contrary. You've done my job for me for so long, it's only fitting that you should finish it. I shan't come to the church.
ISABEL. Serena *will* be disappointed.

(*The sound of African natives singing to their own weird accompaniment is heard off up* R)

Won't you just creep in at the back?

(BLODWEN *bursts in by the upstairs archway. She is dressed in cloak and fur hat.* JASON *moves to* R *of the table above the sofa to watch her*)

BLODWEN (*over the balcony; breathlessly*) A party of natives is at the back door, brandishing spears and makin' strange sounds in their throats.

(JASON *moves to the french windows*)

ISABEL. The Kahooties!

BLODWEN (*coming down the stairs*) Lyin' on the lawn they are, flat on their backs with their legs in the air—you never seen anything like it.

JASON. Sabotage! Someone must have altered the time-table.

(JASON *exits up* R. SIR WILLIAM *moves up* C)

ISABEL (*crossing to the fireplace*) It's all right, Blodwen. It's some friends of my husband's, come for the wedding celebrations.

BLODWEN (*crossing below the sofa to* C) I do not think so. One has a French horn which he beats like a drum, and when I shout, "Who are you?" he grins wide and says, "Benjamin Britten, Benjamin Britten." (*She crosses and stands above Isabel at the fireplace*)

(*The native singing fades.*

BARBARA *enters by the upstairs archway. She wears her bridesmaid's outfit and has the garland around her neck*)

BARBARA (*excitedly*) She's coming! She's coming. (*She comes quickly down the stairs and stands up* R *of the table above the sofa*)

(JASON *enters up* R *and stands below the pillar* RC. *He carries his top hat*)

JASON (*quietly*) The cars are here, my dear.

(*The sky starts to brighten.* ISABEL *moves to* R *of the easy chair.* SIR WILLIAM *crosses to the foot of the stairs.*

SERENA *enters by the upstairs archway. She wears her bridal gown.*

MISS BOWDEN *follows Serena on, carrying her train. All eyes are upon* SERENA *as she comes slowly down the stairs*)

SIR WILLIAM (*to Serena; moved*) You look—very lovely.

(*As* SERENA *reaches the bottom step,* SIR WILLIAM *kisses her on the forehead and gently lowers the bridal veil. He steps back and* SERENA *crosses below the sofa and goes up* C. MISS BOWDEN *follows her.* ISABEL *moves to* R *of Jason.* BARBARA *moves behind the table above the sofa.* SERENA *stands* L *of Jason*)

JASON (*to Serena; quietly*) It's not so bad, you know. Not so bad. (*He kisses Isabel, then offers Serena his arm*)

(SERENA, JASON *and* MISS BOWDEN *exit up* R. ISABEL *moves to the french windows.* BLODWEN *weeps silently into her handkerchief.* BARBARA *moves to* R *of the sofa*)

BARBARA (*to Sir William; confidentially*) I say, if I get scared the night before I'm committed, you might tell them to send me Michelangelo, would you? (*She sees Blodwen in tears, crosses to her, takes the garland from her own neck and puts it carefully around Blodwen's neck*) Never mind. One day, you, too.

BLODWEN. And the sooner the better, isn't it?

(BARBARA *exits up* R.

BLODWEN *follows her off, hopefully. There is a pause*)

ISABEL (*presently; turning to Sir William*) Well, my dear man, I don't know how, but you've done it, and I'm sure there's rejoicing up there. Look, the sun's coming out. I—I take it we shan't meet again.

SIR WILLIAM (*firmly*) Oh, yes, we shall.

(ISABEL *looks puzzled.* SIR WILLIAM *looks upward.* ISABEL *follows his gaze and starts*)

ISABEL. Oh! Quite! (*She beams*) Well in that case, I shall look forward to a good old gossip when I reach the hereafter. And to think that I wasn't altogether sure there was a hereafter heretofore.

JASON (*off; calling*) Isabel, we're waiting.

ISABEL (*calling*) Coming. (*To Sir William. Sincerely*) Well, I must go. Good-bye. And bless you—bless you for everything. Everything.

(ISABEL *exits up* R. *The telephone rings.* SIR WILLIAM *moves to the telephone and lifts the receiver*)

SIR WILLIAM (*into the telephone*) Hullo?

(*An ecclesiastical voice comes from the receiver*)

VOICE (*off; through the telephone*) Good morning. St John's Vicarage. The Vicar speaking.

SIR WILLIAM. Oh, yes, Vicar?

VOICE. I gather you are in some distress.

SIR WILLIAM. No. There—there *was* a problem. It's been solved.

VOICE. Then I take it the bride . . .?

SIR WILLIAM. The bride is—on her way. (*He replaces the receiver, moves to the easy chair, sits, takes a pen and cheque book from his pocket and fills in a cheque*)

(MISS BOWDEN *enters up* R, *moves to* R *of Sir William and stands watching him and smiling*)

(*He tears out the cheque and rises*) This is not the way I should have liked to repay you—but it's the only way I have. Oh, you'll observe I've back-dated it four days. I don't think you'll have any difficulty. (*He holds out the cheque*)

(MISS BOWDEN *takes the cheque and crosses to* C)

At least you'll be comfortable for the rest of your days.

MISS BOWDEN (*toying with the cheque; innocently*) How would you want to "repay" me, Will, if you could?

SIR WILLIAM. I would very much like to have asked you to become my wife.

Miss Bowden (*turning to him; simply*) Ask me, then—go on—just for ducks. I'd like to hear it. Still scared?

Sir William. No, of course not. Nellie Bowden, will you be my lawful wedded wife?

Miss Bowden (*warmly*) Aye—I will an' all.

(Sir William *chuckles and faces front*)

Well, we won't need this *where we've both come from, will we?* (*She smiles broadly, tears up the cheque and throws the pieces on to the sofa*)

(Sir William *turns and stares at her*)

Aye, I went up last night. Didn't they tell you? I'd just left the gown for our lass, and I was crossing the road in a sort of a dream, like, when—you could have knocked me down with a feather. Well, it was one of them Army lorries, actually. They don't give you much time to get settled in up there, though, do they? Do you know, I'd only just started to unpack when the call came through, and back I had to come. Some rule about spinsters, they said—and technically that's me, of course. I nearly died! (*She moves up* C)

(*The french windows open of their own accord. Distant church bells are heard.* Sir William *moves down* R, *turns and faces up* C)

(*She calls upwards*) We're ready when you are.

(*A brilliant white light beams down outside the french windows and shines full on* Miss Bowden's *upturned face*)

(*To Sir William*) They say that's where marriages are made—up yonder. Looks like we really were meant for each other, doesn't it? You one day, me the next. (*She holds out both her hands*) Come on, love. Let's get weaving.

The church bells swell triumphantly as Sir William *slowly moves up* C *to Miss Bowden, as if drawn by some invisible power.* Miss Bowden *turns* R *into the light.* Sir William *puts his hand on her shoulder and they both walk off* R *together into eternity. The lights fade to* Black-Out *as—*

the Curtain *slowly falls*

FINALE

The sound of the bells continues. When the Curtain *is down, the lights come up. The easy chair is moved* R. *A tray with eight glasses of champagne is set on the right end of the table above the sofa, and a wedding cake at the left end.* Miss Bowden *enters by the french windows and goes down* RC. Blodwen *enters down* R *and stands* R *of Miss Bowden.* Barbara, Joe *and* Serena *enter up* R *and stand down* LC. Joe *is now dressed in a morning suit.*

Act III THE BRIDE AND THE BACHELOR 77

When the CURTAIN *rises,* JOE *has just finished arranging Serena's train.*
SIR WILLIAM *enters by the french windows, moves to Serena, kisses her,
shakes hands with Joe, then crosses to* R. JASON *then enters up* R,
moves to Serena, kisses her, shakes hands with Joe, then crosses to R.
ISABEL *enters by the french windows, moves to Serena and Joe, kisses
them both, then crosses to* C, *pushing* BARBARA, *who expects a kiss,
away down* L. *All bow in line,* ISABEL C *with* SIR WILLIAM R *of her
and* JASON L *of her.*

The CURTAIN *falls*

As soon as the CURTAIN *is down, they all go quickly to the table above
the sofa and each collects a glass of champagne to toast the bride and
bridegroom.*

When the CURTAIN *rises, they are all talking and laughing around the
table, with their backs to the audience. After a moment,* ISABEL *turns,
sees they are "discovered", and brings the Company down to take their
calls, glasses in hand. They raise them in a toast to the audience.*

FINAL CURTAIN

FURNITURE AND PROPERTY LIST

ACT I

SCENE 1

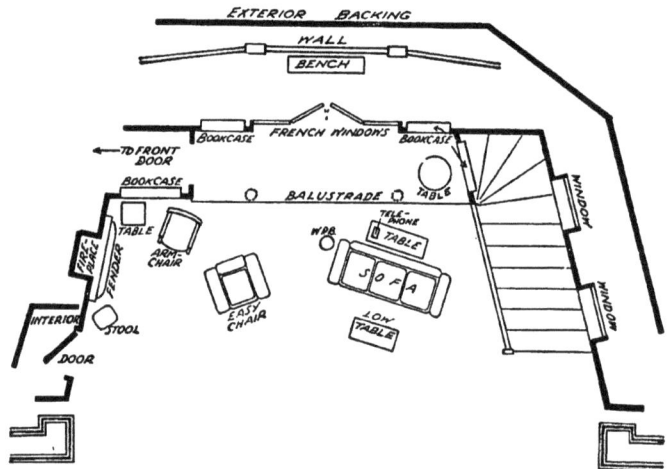

On stage—Sofa. *On it:* cushions, book *From Here to Eternity*, Isabel's handbag
　　　　　　In it: lighter, case with cigarettes
Easy chair (RC)
Coffee table. *On it:* half-eaten apple, plate with 12 sandwiches, ashtray, matches
Table (behind sofa). *On it:* telephone, Isabel's glasses, pair of scissors, 2 corded wood boxes, 1 with pottery and card, 1 with skull and card, copy of the *Evening Standard*, 2 registered envelopes, 1 with Camel brooch, 1 with Pyramid, 2 unopened parcels, small speaker wrapped as parcel
Table (up L). *On it:* table-lamp, 3 parcels, bottle of whisky, syphon of soda, South Africa sherry bottle with cap, ¾ full, sherry decanter, funnel, 4 sherry glasses, 6 whisky glasses
Armchair (up R). *On it:* cushion
Table (up R). *On it:* table-lamp
Fur-covered stool. *On it:* 3 copies of the *Evening Standard*, magazines
Bookshelves (up R). *On them:* native ornaments, books
Bookshelves (up RC). *On them:* oriental ornaments, vases, books
Bookshelves (up LC). *On them:* ornaments, books
Bookshelves (up L). *On them:* vase, books including *Doors of Perception* and *First Steps in Spell-binding*

78

THE BRIDE AND THE BACHELOR

On wall R *and* L *of bookshelves up* L: 2 carved wooden figures
On wall L: 2 wooden carved African masks
On window sills: wooden carved African figures
On balcony wall up L: pair of Eastern stick marionettes
Window curtains
Over mantelpiece: African shield with spears
On mantelpiece: African bust c, pair wooden figures R and L, 2 Chinese bowls, 6 small parcels, 12 invitation cards, framed photograph of Serena, framed photograph of Barbara
Fire basket with fire
Fender
Hearth rug
Carpet on floor
Switches up R
Switches down L
4 wall-brackets
On floor L *of table up* L: 3 large parcels
On newel post: Serena's duffel coat
On floor R *of sofa:* waste-paper basket (full)
On terrace: bench. *On it:* watering can
            Under it: 5 flower pots

Window curtains closed
French windows closed
Door down R closed
Wall-brackets on
Fire on
Lamp up L on
Lamp up R on

Off stage—Dress box, umbrella (MISS BOWDEN)
    Scimitar (ISABEL)
    Mummy case (JASON)
    Book (BLODWEN)
    Spear, brass ring, wooden bowl, garland of flowers, parchment book (JASON)

Personal—JASON: pocket-book and pencil

SCENE 2

Strike—Plate of sandwiches
    Spear
    Scimitar
    Pottery box from under table
    Isabel's handbag
    Duffel coat

Move—Mummy case to clear window curtains

Check—Bowl on coffee table

Window curtains closed
French windows closed
Door down R closed
Wall-brackets off
Fire on
Table-lamps off

Off stage—Garland (BARBARA)
    Knobkerrie (ISABEL)
    Plate with 4 sandwiches (SERENA)

Personal—ISABEL: ear-rings

ACT II

Strike—Knobkerrie
  Replace *First Steps in Spell-binding* in bookcase up L
  Whisky glass from floor R of easy chair
Move—Whisky bottle from mantelpiece to table behind sofa
Set—Clean whisky glass on coffee table

Window curtains open
French windows closed
Door down R open
Wall-brackets on
Fire on
Table-lamps on

Off stage—Glass (SIR WILLIAM)
  Plate with chop, tomatoes, potato-salad, knife and fork (SIR WILLIAM)
  2 full hot-water bottles (JASON)
  Tray. *On it:* beaker of hot milk (JASON)
  Full bottle Canadian whisky (JOE)
  Jason's spectacles (BARBARA)
Personal—JASON: watch
  SIR WILLIAM: pocket scissors, pocket-book, pencil, handkerchief, notes of speech, carnation, cheque-book, pen

ACT III

Strike—Coffee table
  Dirty glasses
  Tray with beaker
  Pot and registered envelopes from mantelpiece
  Joe's jacket
  Mummy case
  Waste-paper basket
  Plate of sandwiches
  Parchment book
  Parcels, string, etc.
  Scissors
  Brass ring
  Cigarette case and lighter
  Book—*Doors of Perception*
  Hot-water bottles

Replace bottles on table up L
Tidy papers on stool down R
Empty ashtrays
Generally tidy room

Set—Clean glasses on table up L
  Index telephone pad on table behind sofa
  Vacuum cleaner, plugged in and practical
  On left arm of sofa: copy of *The Times*
  On right arm of sofa: copy of the *Tatler*
  Wooden bowl on floor down R

Window curtains open
French windows closed
Door down R closed
Wall-brackets off
Table-lamps off
Fire on

THE BRIDE AND THE BACHELOR 81

Off stage—Duster (BLODWEN)
        Copy of the *Daily Mail* (BARBARA)
        Wet umbrella (MISS BOWDEN)
        Cup of coffee (SIR WILLIAM)
        Tray. *On it:* 8 glasses champagne
        Wedding cake
Personal—ISABEL: dark glasses, handkerchief
        MISS BOWDEN: handbag. *In it:* handkerchief, watch
        JOE: wrist-watch
        BLODWEN: handkerchief
        SIR WILLIAM: pen, cheque-book.

LIGHTING PLOT

Property Fittings Required—4 wall-brackets, fire and fire spot, two table-lamps, loud speaker telephone effect

Interior. A lounge-hall. The same scene throughout
THE APPARENT SOURCES OF LIGHT ARE—in daytime—french windows up C and two windows L; at night, 2 wall-brackets R, 1 wall-bracket up L and 1 wall-bracket down L
THE MAIN ACTING AREAS ARE—C, up C, on a sofa RC, at an easy chair RC, on a balcony up C and on the stairs L

ACT I SCENE 1 An October evening

To open: Blue outside windows
        Strips outside arch up R
            outside upstairs arch
            and door down R, on
        Wall-brackets on
        Fire on
        Table-lamp up L on
        Table-lamp up R off

Cue 1 JASON switches on table-lamp up R (page 16)
        Snap in table-lamp
        Snap in light to cover

ACT I SCENE 2 Night

To open: Blue outside windows
        The stage in darkness
        Strips outside arch up R
            outside upstairs arch
            and door down R, off
        Wall-brackets off
        Table-lamps off
        Fire on, dimmed

Cue 2 After scream off   (page 19)
        Snap on strip outside upstairs arch

Cue 3 SERENA switches on wall-brackets   (page 19)
        Snap in wall-brackets
        Snap in onstage lights

Cue 4 ISABEL switches off wall-brackets   (page 21)
        Snap out wall-brackets
        Snap out onstage lights

Cue 5	ISABEL exits *Snap out strip outside upstairs arch*	(page 22)
Cue 6	SERENA switches on table-lamp up L *Snap in table-lamp up L* *Snap in lights to cover*	(page 22)
Cue 7	SERENA : ". . . candy floss." *Snap on strip outside upstairs arch*	(page 23)
Cue 8	ISABEL switches on wall-brackets *Snap in wall-brackets* *Snap in onstage lights*	(page 23)

ACT II Night

To open: Blue outside windows
Strips outside arch up R
      outside upstairs arch
      and door down R, on
Wall-brackets on
Table-lamps on
Fire on, dimmed

Cue 9	SIR WILLIAM: ". . . living proof." *Flash of lightning*	(page 52)
Cue 10	ISABEL: ". . . thunderbolt." *Several flashes of lightning*	(page 52)
Cue 11	ISABEL: "How dare you!" *Lightning flashes*	(page 54)

ACT III Morning

To open: Effect of a thin watery light
Strips outside arch up R
      outside upstairs arch
      and door down R, on
Wall-brackets off
Table-lamps off
Fire on

Cue 12	BARBARA: "She's coming!" *Bring up lighting for sunshine effect*	(page 74)
Cue 13	MISS BOWDEN: "We're ready when you are." *Focus brilliant white spot on Miss Bowden*	(page 76)
Cue 14	SIR WILLIAM and MISS BOWDEN exit *Dim all lights to* BLACK-OUT	(page 76)
Cue 15	When CURTAIN is down *Bring up stage lighting to full*	(page 76)

EFFECTS PLOT

ACT I

SCENE 1

Cue 1	BARBARA: ". . . breathe deeply." *Door bell rings, followed by rat-a-tat-tat on front door*	(page 2)
Cue 2	ISABEL: "Serena!" *Telephone rings*	(page 5)

Cue 3	BLODWEN: ". . . be appreciated." *Telephone rings*	(page 10)
Cue 4	ISABEL: "Hallo?" *Sound of jazz music through the telephone. This continues until the end of the telephone conversation*	(page 10)
Cue 5	ISABEL: "I beg your pardon." *Sound of African drumming gradually increasing in volume*	(page 13)
Cue 6	JASON: ". . . Shepherd's Bush." *Loud knocking on front door*	(page 13)
Cue 7	ISABEL: ". . . right behind him." *Knocking on front door*	(page 14)
Cue 8	ISABEL: "Charge!" *The drumming ceases*	(page 14)

SCENE 2

Cue 9	After rise of CURTAIN *Scream off*	(page 19)
Cue 10	ISABEL: ". . . wisdom of the ages." *Distant clock strikes midnight*	(page 21)
Cue 11	ISABEL exits *Sound of wind. This continues until SIR WILLIAM has entered*	(page 22)

ACT II

Cue 12	JASON: ". . . pointed distinctly to . . ." *Distant clock strikes one*	(page 29)
Cue 13	SIR WILLIAM: ". . . living proof." *Clap of thunder follows lightning*	(page 52)
Cue 14	JASON: ". . . by thunder." *Crash of thunder follows lightning*	(page 52)
Cue 15	SIR WILLIAM: ". . . Garden of Eden." *Roll of thunder*	(page 52)
Cue 16	ISRAEL: ". . . thunderbolt." *Terrific clap of thunder*	(page 52)
Cue 17	ISABEL: "How dare you!" *Thunder crashes*	(page 54)

ACT III

Cue 18	At rise of CURTAIN *Sound of wailing wind*	(page 55)
Cue 19	ISABEL: ". . . right as rain." *A sudden gust of wind*	(page 56)
Cue 20	BLODWEN: ". . . King's Evil." *A sudden gust of wind, then fade to out*	(page 56)
Cue 21	BARBARA: "Willie's not evil." *Sound of wind*	(page 58)
Cue 22	ISABEL: ". . . he's had it." *A big gust of wind*	(page 58)
Cue 23	ISABEL: "Ha!" *The wind fades*	(page 58)
Cue 24	SIR WILLIAM: ". . . gift completely." *The wind starts gently*	(page 64)

Cue 25	ISABEL holds the bowl at the french windows *A great gust of wind*	(page 65)
Cue 26	ISABEL: ". . . we've had our quota . . ." *The wind fades*	(page 65)
Cue 27	SIR WILLIAM: "That's marriage." *The telephone rings*	(page 70)
Cue 28	ISABEL: ". . . calling long distance?" *Crackling sounds through the telephone*	(page 70)
Cue 29	ISABEL: ". . . crackling noise——" *Swishing sound through the telephone*	(page 70)
Cue 30	ISABEL: ". . . blasting of wind, as if . . ." *Maroon sound through the telephone*	(page 70)
Cue 31	SIR WILLIAM: ". . . to be seen." *The telephone rings*	(page 72)
Cue 32	ISABEL: ". . . be disappointed." *The sound of African natives singing to their own weird accompaniment*	(page 73)
Cue 33	BLODWEN: ". . . Benjamin Britten." *The native singing fades*	(page 74)
Cue 34	ISABEL: "Everything." *The telephone rings*	(page 75)
Cue 35	MISS BOWDEN: "I nearly died." *Distant sound of church bells*	(page 76)
Cue 36	MISS BOWDEN: "Let's get weaving" *The sound of the bells swells up*	(page 76)

NOTES

Telephone Effect

This consists of a battery-operated telephone from off stage to on stage with a hand microphone feeding through a small amplifier to the "parcel" speaker on stage. The Artist uses the Stage handset in the ordinary way and can hear the offstage conversation through his handset and the artist off stage can hear the onstage conversation. The audience consequently only hear the offstage conversation through the "parcel speaker". A single turntable feeds the piano effect through the small amplifier to the "parcel" speaker, at the same time the offstage conversation can be heard.

The staircase and balcony are an integral part of this acting edition, and a desirable element in any production, but the design can be modified to a few steps and an archway, if necessary.

MADE AND PRINTED IN GREAT BRITAIN BY
LATIMER TREND & COMPANY LTD PLYMOUTH
MADE IN ENGLAND

www.ingramcontent.com/pod-product-compliance
Ingram Content Group UK Ltd.
Pitfield, Milton Keynes, MK11 3LW, UK
UKHW021840210426
5322IPUK00022B/385